T0004117

Healthy, Delicious and Affordable
85 Mix-and-Match Bento-Box Recipes

ULTIMATE
BENTO

Marc Matsumoto
Maki Ogawa

TUTTLE Publishing

Tokyo | Rutland, Vermont | Singapore

Contents

Yakitori Grilled Chicken Bento, page 76

Hamburger Cutlet Bento, page 64   Loco Moco Hamburg Steak Bento, page 56   Takikomi Tuna Rice Bento, page 84

The Recipes

Omurice Bento, page 158   Hanami Bento, page 126   Summer Roll Bento, page 92

Chili Shrimp Bento, page 144

Chicken Nanban Bento, page 88

Kushiage Chicken Skewer Bento, page 130

The Joys of Bento

Bento lunch boxes are often associated with the Japanese culture of cuteness, but a daily bento-lunch habit can be about so much more. A vibrant, balanced bento that's packed with love not only nourishes your body and cuts back on spending, but it's a turning point that can transform a lousy morning into a joyful afternoon.

Marc Introduces Himself and Maki

I was born in Japan, but my mother and I moved to the United States when I was six months old. When Mom remarried, we moved to a rural agricultural town in Northern California, where there weren't many kids that looked like me. Far from my roots and in a mixed-ethnicity household, my only connection to Japan was the comforting Japanese food my mother would cook for my sister, stepfather and me. It was through her cooking that I learned about Japanese culture and traditions. Although I couldn't speak the language, by the time I left home I was able to cook a balanced, healthful meal based on the fundamentals of Japanese cuisine.

Maki and her younger brother were born and raised in Saitama, Japan. Their mother worked full time, and by the time Maki was in high school, she was splitting cooking duties for the family with her father, who loves cooking — he helped guide Maki's first steps in the kitchen. In tenth grade, Maki started packing her own bento box for lunch. Her first attempt was nothing more than burnt sausages, a misshapen *tamagoyaki* rolled omelet and rice, but through the daily ritual of packing and eating her bento lunches she developed an early understanding of not just the basics of cooking, but of the emotional power of food.

The two of us may have had vastly different childhoods, but we both grew into adults with an appreciation for the ability of food to act as a means of communication with those around us.

Maki and I first met as co-hosts of a popular international television show about bento. Maki had become an established bento expert through her own experiences as a mom of two sons. My love of eating had morphed into a passion for cooking, and I'd left my desk job to share my experiences in the kitchen through No Recipes, my paradoxically named blog. Over our five seasons of hosting the show together, we've heard stories from around the world about the impact that making bento lunches has had on people's lives. By writing this book, Maki and I hope to help you discover the joys of making a bento, regardless of your background or experience.

The Bento Ritual

For both of us, packing a bento has become a regular ritual. The satisfaction it offers is a bit like wrapping a birthday present that we know our loved ones will enjoy.

When Maki's eldest son had a difficult time adjusting to life in preschool, she got into the habit of making regular bento lunches for him. Leaving home with a bento box packed with cute characters and the joy of opening his bento at lunchtime made school something to look forward to. A crowd would gather to look at his fun bento lunches, which also gave him a chance to make friends.

By the time her younger son started school, Maki thought she'd mastered the art of making lunchtime fun for kids. But as most parents know, kids (just like grown-ups) can have very different personalities. Unlike her oldest child, her younger son was embarrassed by the cute characters in his bento and would try to hide the contents of his lunch as he ate. By changing the way she packed his bento, she was able to create a lunchtime experience that was as satisfying for him as it was for his older brother!

I first started making bento in the US as a way to save money. I didn't own any bento boxes, but I did have a lot of plastic food-storage containers. These are a great way to start off; most people already have at least a few sitting around, and they provide a blank canvas to express your culinary creativity without any distractions. Perhaps these humble beginnings instilled a belief in me that bento is more about the food and how it's presented than the box itself.

These days, I have a young daughter who loves helping me in the kitchen, and she enjoys packing her own bento. How you eat as a child and what you learn about food during childhood, has a lifelong impact on health and happiness. Packing a balanced bento with a child is a great way to introduce concepts such as balancing macronutrients (carbohydrates, fat, protein and water), portion control, and "eating the rainbow" (one way to identify micronutrients).

As these anecdotes demonstrate, a bento isn't just about making cute things out of food, or

packing it into a fancy box; it's about creating a nourishing meal that everybody can enjoy.

How to Use This Book

In the following pages, you'll learn how to plan, cook and pack your bento. Although the space is limited, we've tried to cram all our collective experience into this fun guide.

In the first section of the book, you'll learn all about the different types of bento boxes (page 14), as well as the accessories, tools and utensils that can help you streamline your daily bento making (page 18). The important thing to remember here is that these are just aids, and are not necessary for making a bento. Some of Maki's most-used tools are repurposed objects from around the house, including straws of different sizes, which she uses to cut out circles of ham, cheese, etc., for decorative elements. It's not difficult to assemble a set of tools without spending a ton of money.

In the first section, we also provide lots of useful tips on packing (page 22) and food safety (page 26), as well as ideas for planning ahead and shopping for your bento (page 28). For those who are new to Japanese cuisine, you'll find a glossary of some of the key ingredients we'll be using for the recipes in this book (page 30). Although many Japanese sauces can be purchased premade, most are easy to make at home, and they can be made ahead, so we've also included a section with basic instructions for making sauces and other basic recipes that you can use again and again.

Although Maki and I both agree that a bento isn't just about cuteness, making attractive decorations that add a touch of *kawaii* to your bento and joy to your heart can be quick and easy. Maki has written an entire section on decorations (see pages 40 to 49) to help you turn everyday ingredients into cute characters and accents. These can be added to any bento to bring it to life.

The main part of the book, from page 50 onwards, contains recipes for 25 complete bento-box menus. These are a mix of classic and modern Japanese dishes, and while they're a good starting place, you don't have to assemble the bento boxes exactly as we do. In fact, we encourage you to read this book out of sequence, mixing and matching various main courses, rice dishes and sides to come up with your own unique bento-box combinations. We hope these ideas spark inspiration, but most importantly, we hope you experience the joys of bento making!

Maki and I are looking forward to seeing the creative bentos you come up with, so be sure to follow us @norecipes and @cuteobento on Instagram and tag your photos with #UltimateBento!

The Boxes

The Japanese word *bento* (弁当) refers to the traditional Japanese lunch box as well as the meal that it contains. These days there are many styles of bento box, and in this section, we're going to outline the most common materials used to make bento boxes along with the different shapes and sizes they come in. The goal is to give you enough expertise to make informed decisions about the containers that will work best for the types of lunch that you want to pack.

Wood

Wood is the material originally used to make traditional Japanese bento boxes. Wooden bento boxes are beautiful and surprisingly light. Because wood is the most porous bento-box material, using a wooden bento box helps avoid the condensation that can make the rice in your bento soggy.

This ability to breathe has its drawbacks, though: wooden bento boxes are prone to staining and retaining odors. This is also why wooden bento boxes aren't well suited for meals that contain sauces or liquids — the wood can absorb the moisture and warp or even crack.

Lacquered wooden bento boxes can usually be identified by their glossy red or black finish. The lacquer seals the wood, making it more resistant to damage from moisture. These containers tend to be expensive and fragile, however, which is why lacquered bento boxes are usually reserved for special occasions. These days, melamine plastic is an alternative material used to make this style of bento box. It can closely mimic the look of lacquered wood without the drawbacks.

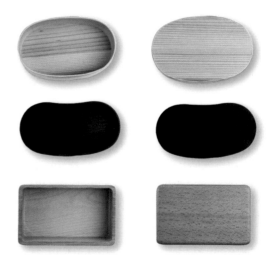

Wooden bento boxes

If you do decide to use a wooden bento box, be aware that it needs to be washed and thoroughly dried as soon as you are done eating. In addition, wooden bento boxes should never be washed in a dishwasher.

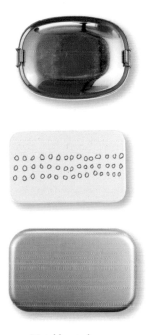

Metal bento boxes

Plastic bento boxes

Metal

They cannot be microwaved, but metal bento boxes won't take on stains or odors, so foods with intense colors and flavors such as beets or curry can be packed without worrying about ruining the container. When cared for properly, metal bento boxes can last a lifetime.

Aluminum boxes are lightweight and durable, but they tend to scratch easily and should not be used to hold acidic foods. They should also never be washed in a dishwasher.

Stainless-steel bento boxes are a little heavier than aluminum, but they are less reactive and are generally dishwasher safe.

Enameled metal boxes are coated in a layer of glass that makes them non-reactive and scratch-resistant. They are typically dishwasher safe; however, they tend to be heavy, and the coating can shatter and flake off if the container is dropped.

Plastic

Lightweight, inexpensive and available in many colors and shapes, most modern bento boxes are made from plastic. They are unlikely to break, but plastic containers scratch easily, which can cause them to retain stains and odors, limiting their lifespan. Some plastics are also prone to warping at high temperatures, so you should check the manufacturer's specifications before microwaving plastic bento boxes or washing them in the dishwasher.

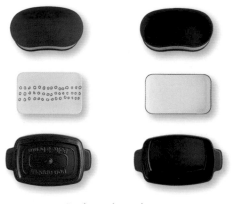

Single-tier bento boxes

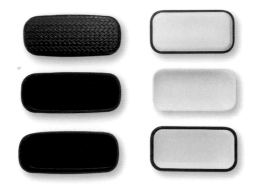

Double-tier bento boxes

Single Tier

Most bento boxes are single-tier boxes in various shapes and sizes, with one large compartment that can be divided as you like. Single-tier boxes are great for accommodating large bento items like a slice of salmon or a steak. The larger unpartitioned space requires a bit of planning and thought to keep flavors separate while making everything fit, but these are the most flexible bento boxes that can be used for almost any kind of bento.

Double Tier

Two-tiered bento boxes have a smaller footprint, but they are also taller due to the stacked design. Depending on how you are transporting them, this can make them easier to carry, and they don't take as much space in your kitchen cabinet when not in use. They also allow for a clear separation of colors, tastes and smells, so you can pack sweet things in one box and savory foods in the other. The downside is that each tier is quite small, so it may take a bit of creativity to make the most of the space. Two-tiered boxes also give you the flexibility

to pack your bento in two stages. For instance, you would normally wait for hot foods to cool completely before adding them to your bento box, but with a two-tier box, you can put the hot foods in one tier and let them cool in the box (without closing the lid) while you pack the other tier.

Baskets

Baskets are not only visually appealing, their woven design makes them light while letting air circulate through the box. When lined with dried bamboo

Baskets

Donburi bento boxes

Food storage containers

leaves, or parchment paper, they are particularly well suited for rice dishes as well as sandwiches, because the open design of the box keeps the food from getting soggy. Baskets, however, are not well suited for foods that will release liquid over time such as fruit and vegetables with a high moisture content.

Donburi

Donburi-style bento boxes are essentially bowls with a lid, perfect for packing rice-bowl dishes such as Chicken and Egg Soboro Bento (page 148) and Tempura Donburi Bento (page 136), as well as noodle dishes. Since these bento boxes are made to hold a single main-course dish, they are easier to pack and eat than bento boxes that contain multiple items. Some donburi containers are thermally insulated with a screw-top lid, which allows you to transport hot soups and stews.

Food Storage Containers

What they lack in style, food storage containers make up for in their accessibility and flexibility.

Available in a wide variety of shapes and sizes, you can choose the right one for the food you plan to pack. For example, you may decide to pack foods you plan to reheat in one container while you pack fruits and veggies in a separate smaller container. Food storage containers also have the benefit of having a tight-fitting lid that is not easily dislodged, preventing spills while you're on the move. If you're new to bento making, these are the perfect stepping stone before you go out and buy yourself a dedicated bento box.

Partitioned (Western style)

While these Western-style bento boxes make it very easy to separate the different components of your bento, ready-partitioned bento boxes are not commonly used in Japan outside of the food-service industry. Maki and I aren't fans of this style of bento box because they take up a lot of space, and limit how the bento can be packed. Bento boxes need to be packed tightly so that food doesn't shift in transit, and it usually takes far more food than one person can eat to pack a partitioned bento box tightly.

Useful Tools and Accessories

Over time, every bento maker collects a drawer full of utensils, cutters, molds and improvised tools for making and packing bento boxes. In this section, we're going to cover the basic tools we will be using in this book. If you're just starting out, you don't need a lot of fancy gadgets to make a bento. Get creative by repurposing other tools or objects you may have around the house already. If you do choose to improvise, please be sure the items you are using are clean and safe for use with food.

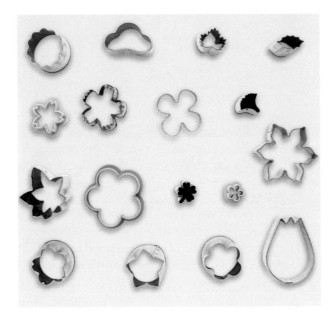

Cutters When decorating a bento, it helps to have tools to cut out foods such as vegetables, egg, nori sheets and cheese. You can use dedicated vegetable and nori cutters, but other tools, like scissors and small cookie cutters, work as well. You can also get creative; for example, use straws of varying diameters to cut circles and ovals in food.

Flowers Using small flower-shaped cutters to cut vegetables such as carrots, daikon radish and sweet potatoes is a great way to add a fun splash of color to a bento box. In Japan, where different flowers represent different seasons, the shape of the flower used can give your bento a seasonal touch. These cutters can also be used in creative ways, such as using a daffodil cutter to make snowflakes (see page 42), or a plum-blossom cutter to make butterflies (see page 41).

Leaves Leaves are another element used to convey a sense of the season in Japan. Cutting yellow and orange vegetables into leaf shapes can help you create a fall scene in your bento.

Shapes Whether they're circles, hearts, stars or triangles, small cutters in these standard shapes can be used in various combinations to make almost anything. For example, a heart turned upside-down can become the snout of a seal or a triangle cut out from the top of a circle can become a fox's face.

Cups

It's typically not a great idea to add foods with a lot of liquid to a bento box, but if you must, using small cups is one way to stop these items from spilling. Cups can also be used to keep foods such as fruit or dessert separate from the savory parts of your bento box. To minimize waste, we recommend using reusable plastic or silicone cups.

Partitions

To keep the flavors of different foods in a bento box from mixing, some people like to add plastic or paper partitions to their bento box. Maki and I prefer using edible leaves to partition off different components of a bento. These add a splash of color and a boost in nutrients while avoiding waste.

Picks

Decorative picks can be handy for picking up small pieces of food and are a quick way to make a bento box more colorful. If your bento box is packed with a nutritionally balanced rainbow of colors, though, they're unnecessary.

Sauce bottles

If you add sauce to one of your bento dishes when packing, it may turn soggy by lunch time. Try packing your sauce separately in a small bottle, so that you can add it to your dish just before eating.

Toothpicks These can be useful for precise placement of small decorative details such as dots of nori. They can also be used to carve shapes out of a thin slice of cheese — just insert the tip into the cheese and run it along the desired path at a 45° angle.

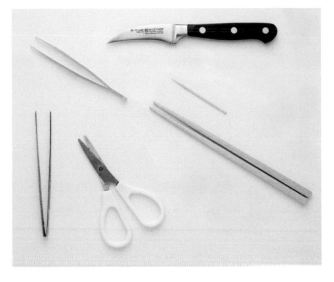

Tweezers Clean tweezers are useful for placing small details onto your bento with precision.

Chopsticks You can cook and eat your bento with spatulas, forks, knives and spoons, but why not try your hand with chopsticks? In Japan chopsticks are used for everything from whisking to stir-frying to eating. Cooking chopsticks are typically longer and thicker than those used for eating, and made of uncoated wood to keep your hands safe and your food free of plastic or lacquer. Chopsticks used for plating and packing tend to have very thin tips and require a bit of skill to use, but they allow you to place food with pinpoint precision. Finally, chopsticks meant for eating are shorter, and are often textured near the tips to help you grip the food you're picking up.

Paring knife Having a small paring knife is useful for peeling and cutting fruits and vegetables to fit in a bento box. It is also very handy for trimming and carving small details into the foods you add.

Small kitchen scissors A small pair of dedicated kitchen scissors can be useful for hand cutting shapes from nori sheets, or for trimming leafy greens down to the proper size to use as a partition.

Nonstick frying pan While nonstick frying pans are nice to have for many dishes, they are essential for egg dishes such as tamagoyaki-style Rainbow Omelet (page 142) or Egg Crepe (page 160).

Deep pot If you don't have a rice cooker, a deep pot or saucepan is a must when making rice to keep it from boiling over. A deep pot is also useful for boiling vegetables and making sauces.

Nori punches In Japan, you can find nori punches sold in different shapes and sizes (see picture above). Such punches may be available in your country at stores selling Japanese products, as well as on online marketplaces and auction sites. While it's best to use tools that are manufactured for use with food, you may find you can use paper punches to achieve a similar result.

Straws Because they come in a variety of sizes, straws are perfect for cutting small details out of cheese, ham or cooked root vegetables. Just press one end into the food to cut out a shape. You can use straws to cut out circles or to cut holes in food. To cut out rings, use a small straw to make a hole inside a circle made by a bigger straw.

Tamagoyaki omelet pan As you'll see in Maki's Grilled Salmon and Omelet Bento (page 140), you can make tamagoyaki omelet without a special pan. However, if you plan on making it regularly, buying a rectangular tamagoyaki pan (pictured above) can save you some time. This pan can also be used to sauté small portions of vegetables for your bento.

Plastic wrap

The nonstick nature of plastic wrap makes it a handy way to mold foods such as rice balls and omelets.

Rubber bands

Rubber bands are useful for marking guidelines for square and rectangle shapes on a bento box.

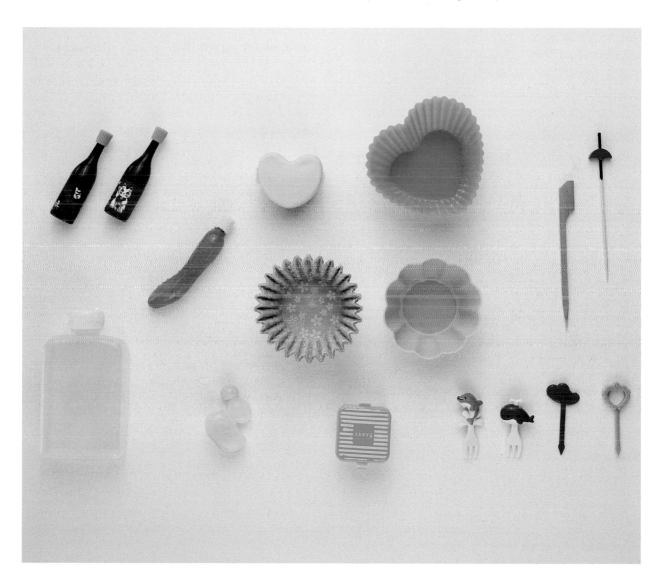

Packing Tips

Although most people associate the word "bento" with the box itself, the art of bento making isn't so much about the container or even about the food inside — it is about how the food is packed. Once you understand the basics of packing a bento, you can make one from practically anything, using almost any container. Traditional Japanese bento boxes always contain rice, protein (usually fish) and pickled vegetables, but these days they often include bread, pasta and meat, as well as fresh vegetables and fruit. Since the definition of bento has evolved in modern times, and there are no hard and fast rules, Maki and I have prepared three simple tips to guide you as you pack your bento.

Taco Rice Bento, page 72.

Tip 1: Make it colorful

The common adage amongst chefs that "first you eat with your eyes" is supported by research showing that visual cues such as color, gloss and shape can alter our perception of taste. A colorful bento can whet a grown-up's appetite, and a fun arrangement of those colors can also get kids to eat foods they usually wouldn't try.

Adding a wide array of colors isn't just about making food more appealing, though. Packing a bento with a rainbow of fruit and vegetables can help you ensure a more balanced array of nutrients. For example, red fruit and veggies are often loaded with lycopene, while orange and yellow ones get their color from carotenoids such as beta-carotene and lutein. Green vegetables are full of carotenoids too, but they also bring folate, fiber, vitamin C and minerals to the party. Blue and purple fruit and vegetables get their color from antioxidants, and even white and brown foods can be a good source of minerals and phytonutrients.

Loco Moco Hamburg Steak Bento, page 56

Chicken and Egg Soboro Bento, page 148

Sukiyaki Beef, Egg & Rice Sandwich, page 110

Karaage Fried Chicken Bento, page 60

Omurice Bento, page 159

Hanami Bento, page 127

Chicken Nanban Bento, page 88

Honey Lemon Chicken Bento, page 98

Ham and Cheese Roll Bento, page 116

Tip 2: Pack it tightly

Japan is a small country with a large population, so whether you're talking about cars, apartments or bento boxes, everything tends to be a little more compact. People often marvel at how dainty Japanese bento boxes are, but most will easily hold more than a pound of food when they are properly packed. The key is to fill the box from edge to edge without leaving any space. This will ensure that there's plenty of food to help you power through the afternoon.

More importantly, packing your bento tightly prevents the contents from shifting around while the box is being carried to work or school. An excellent way to test this is to cover your bento box with its lid and give it a shake from side to side. If the contents of your bento don't shift around, you've packed it well.

Tip 3: Separate the flavors

Given how cozy the food in your bento is going be, you're probably wondering how to stop the flavors mingling. Teriyaki sauce on rice is delicious, but tonkatsu sauce on strawberries is no good. This is where separators come in.

Separators are physical barriers; they can be anything from strips of plastic to muffin cups. Our favorite way of keeping foods separate is to use edible leaves such as kale, lettuce, cabbage and radicchio. Leaves work like bubble wrap to pad your bento and keep things from moving about while maintaining separate areas for different flavors. As a bonus, the leaves add a burst of color and nutrients as well!

Ham and Cheese Roll Bento, page 116

Kushiage Chicken Skewer Bento, page 130

A colorful bento like the Hanami Bento, page 126, can whet a grown-ups appetite and get kids to eat food they wouldn't normally try!

To make sure your bento box stays tightly packed, like this Karaage Fried Chicken Bento, page 60, the key is to fill the box from side to side, without leaving any space.

The Fried Egg and Chicken Meatball Bento, page 52, shows how you can use physical barriers such as salad leaves to maintain separate areas for different flavors.

Bento Food Safety

If several hours are going to pass between making and eating your bento, you need to make sure that the food you have packed does not go off. Here is a list of things you can do to make your bento as safe as possible.

Stuffed Bell Pepper Bento, page 80

Maitake Mushroom Steak Bento, page 152

Miso Butter Chicken Bento, page 106

Cook it This may seem obvious, but I can't tell you how many times I've seen people add raw fish to their bento boxes. Never add raw proteins to a bento box, and make sure any raw fruit or vegetables you add are thoroughly washed.

Make your proteins well done They may be delicious, but rare steaks and runny eggs may go off if packed in a bento box that is not going to be eaten for several hours.

Season well If you've ever found the side dishes in a bento to be salty, it's for a good reason. Salt helps to slow microbial growth. By ensuring your side dishes are well seasoned, you can reduce the chances of them spoiling before you eat them. Lowering the pH (i.e., making the dishes more acidic) is another way of slowing microbial growth, which is why vinegar and lemon juice make for good bento seasonings as well.

Gloves and utensils We recommend washing your hands thoroughly before packing your bento, to avoid contaminating the food. If possible, use clean chopsticks, tongs or tweezers to place food in the bento box, rather than using your hands.

Leftovers It's okay to use last night's leftovers in your bento, but make sure you separate out the portions you plan to pack before you serve your evening meal, and refrigerate them immediately.

Let it cool Covering a warm bento with a lid not only makes it retain heat, but it also causes condensation to form. The extra heat and moisture can lead to spoiling, which is why you always want to make sure the food in your bento box is at room temperature or below before closing it up.

Keep it cool It's important to keep your bento in a cool place until you eat it. A cooler bag with an ice pack is essential if you live in a warm climate.

Keep it clean Although it may be tempting to postpone dealing with your dirty bento box until you get home, you should always try to wash and dry your bento box as soon as you finish eating. This is especially important for boxes made of wood, as the porous material will harbor microbes.

Grilled Salmon and Omelet Bento, page 140

Planning and Shopping

Who doesn't enjoy sitting down to lunch and opening the lid of an elegant bento box to reveal a sumptuous feast within? There's just one problem: someone has to pack that bento. Incorporating bento-making into your daily routine may seem like a high hurdle, but with a little planning, it will fit in seamlessly between brushing your teeth and heading out your front door to take on the day!

Have a Plan

Like most things in life, having a game plan will make integrating bento-making into your morning schedule smoother and stress-free. Assuming you work a regular five-day week, that means setting aside a bit of time on the weekends to create a meal plan for the upcoming week.

The art of meal planning doesn't have to be complicated. Your meal plan could be as simple as dividing a piece of paper into five columns and jotting down your dinner menu for the week. Be sure to include bento-friendly items that you can set aside to pack into your bento the next day.

Shopping

Having a meal plan in hand for the week ahead helps you stay focused on the healthy food you need while grocery shopping, so you're less prone to being distracted by unnecessary junk food. Don't forget to include all the small portions of vegetables or fruit you will use to fill out or partition your bento box.

Both raw and cooked vegetables can be added to a bento, and they often require minimal preparation, which is why I always load my shopping basket up with a rainbow of fresh seasonal veggies.

I also make sure to buy whatever fruit is in season to add to my bento box. It's an easy way to provide an appetizing splash of color, and it doubles as dessert!

To make partitions in your bento box that keep the different types of food separate, you want to keep an eye out for large, colorful leafy greens that can be eaten raw.

Leftovers

Cooking extra food for your next meal is a great way to make your time in the kitchen more efficient. It allows you to double your meal prep efficiency without doubling up on the effort.

One way to do this is to add bento-friendly side dishes to your dinner menu that can be stored for use the next day. For example, you could make a few extra portions of a main dish, or you could drop a few snap peas and carrot flowers into the water you're using to boil the corn you plan on serving for dinner that night. If you're an early riser, a variation on this strategy is to make extra portions of food you're preparing for your bento, which you can then repurpose for dinner that night.

Regardless of which strategy you use, always pack and refrigerate the food you plan to use for your next meal immediately. The longer food is left in the danger zone (between 40°F and 140°F, or 4°C and 60°C), the higher your likelihood of getting ill.

Key Ingredients

Although I now live in Japan, I grew up floating between the US and Australia, and I know how hard it can be to find Japanese ingredients abroad. That's why Maki and I have chosen recipes that use as few specialty ingredients as possible. If you live in a major metropolitan area, you should be able to find most of the ingredients you will need to make the recipes in this book at your local supermarket. We know it can be daunting to work with items you've never used before, so here's a primer on the basic Japanese ingredients we'll be using in this book.

Abura-age fried tofu (油揚げ)
Abura-age, which literally means "oil-fried," refers to thin slices of tofu that have been sliced and double-fried until they puff into fluffy sheets that are a light tan color. The resulting texture is somewhat meatlike, making this a good plant-based source of protein. In Japan, abura-age is often chopped up and used to add both texture and flavor to miso soup and rice dishes, and it's used as a wrapper for the type of sushi called *inari-zushi*. You can find abura-age in Asian grocery stores, usually in the frozen or refrigerated section next to the tofu.

Japanese rice (米) The recipes in this book use Japanese short-grain rice (*Oryza sativa* subsp. japonica), sometimes labeled "sushi rice." Unfortunately most "Japanese-style" rice sold in the US is a medium-grain cultivar called Calrose. All rice contains two types of starch: amylose and amylopectin. The ratio of the two determines the mouth feel of the cooked rice, as well as the texture of the rice once it is cooled. Unlike long-grain rice, Japanese short-grain rice has a high ratio of amylopectin, which is what gives it its sticky texture. The high proportion of amylopectin also allows the rice to stay tender even after it's cooled, making short-grain rice a better option for a bento, as the rice will be tender even if you don't reheat it. The three most common varieties of Japanese short-grain rice that are produced in the US are Koshihikari, Hitomebore and Milky Queen (sold as Yuki No Kakera).

Miso paste (味噌) Japanese miso paste comes in varieties

ranging in color from cream to tan to red to black, depending on how long the miso has been fermented and aged. Lighter varieties of miso can be made in as little as two weeks. At the dark end of the spectrum, the miso can be aged for up to two years.

Nearly all miso is made with soybeans and salt, but most types contain a third ingredient called *koji*. Koji is rice or barley that has been inoculated with *Aspergillus oryzae*, a type of filamentous fungus that aids fermentation. Since barley is not gluten-free, if you are looking for gluten free miso, you'll want to find one that's made with rice koji.

Unless otherwise specified, the recipes in this book use yellow miso, which should be tan to light brown. Outside of Japan, this type of miso is frequently mislabeled "white miso." This is confusing because white miso is an entirely different type of miso that is a creamy light yellow and very sweet, due to the high ratio of rice koji used in its production. Avoid "seasoned miso" or "miso with dashi" as these are intended for making instant miso soup and have additives such as fish and MSG which make them unsuitable for cooking.

Nori sheets (海苔) Nori is a type of algae that is dried into sheets that resemble black paper. Nori sheets are used to wrap foods like sushi and *onigiri* rice balls, and can be used as a garnish. The dark color and paper-like texture make it perfect for cutting with a pair of scissors or a paper punch to create details to add to a bento such as eyes, a nose or a mouth.

Panko bread crumbs (パン粉) *Panko*, literally "bread crumbs" in Japanese, is typically made from the white part of sandwich bread,

making it uniformly white. The texture of panko is coarser and airier than that of Western bread crumbs, so fried foods coated in it have a wonderfully crisp texture. Panko is also used as an additive to minced-meat dishes such as Stuffed Mini Bell Peppers (page 82) and Loco Moco Hamburg Steak (page 58) to keep the meat tender and juicy. Panko can be found relatively easily in the ethnic foods section of most supermarkets. You can also make panko at home by cutting the crusts off stale sandwich bread and pulsing in a food processor until the crumbs are about 1/8 inch (3–4 mm) in diameter.

Potato starch (片栗粉) Known as *katakuriko* in Japan, this powdered starch was originally derived from the corm of the katakuri lily (*Erythronium japonicum*). These days, almost all katakuriko is made from potatoes.

Potato starch is used to thicken sauces, bind ingredients, and coat fried foods such as *karaage* fried chicken. If you can't find potato starch, you can use cornstarch instead, but potato starch will give a smoother texture to your sauces, especially when they are chilled. Potato starch also works better than cornstarch as a coating for fried foods because it creates a lighter, crispier shell.

Rice vinegar (米酢) Rice vinegar, sometimes called "rice wine vinegar," is a mild vinegar made from either rice or the lees left over from making sake. It has a unique flavor and mild acidity, so we do not recommend substituting other types of vinegar. Rice vinegar is available in regular supermarkets and Asian groceries.

Sake (日本酒) Sake is an alcoholic beverage made by using *koji* (*Aspergillus oryzae*) and yeast to ferment rice.

As well as being a popular drink, sake is used extensively in Japanese cuisine as an ingredient, to add umami to foods. Umami is one of the five elements of taste perception, along with salt, sweet, sour and bitter. Although it's often described as "savory," umami can benefit sweet foods like cakes and cookies as well. Sake, in particular, is loaded with the amino acids that stimulate the umami taste receptors in your mouth, making it a great way to boost flavor.

Because of its unique production method and taste, there is no good substitute for sake. Since most, if not all, of the alcohol is burned off during cooking, foods cooked with sake should be safe for children to consume.

If you can't find it or don't want to use it, the best substitute is water.

You don't need to use expensive sake to cook with. However, we recommend avoiding anything labeled "cooking sake." This is produced from either low-grade sake or sake-flavored alcohol, and is loaded with salt (to circumvent alcohol taxation laws). Cooking sake may add off-flavors to your food, and make it too salty.

Sesame oil (ごま油) Sesame oil can be toasted or untoasted. Untoasted sesame oil is yellow with a mild, neutral flavor. It's primarily used in South Asian cuisine. Toasted sesame oil is made by pressing toasted sesame seeds and is amber to medium brown. It has a strong nutty taste and is the type of sesame oil used for all the recipes in this book.

Sesame seeds (煎り胡麻) In Japan, sesame seeds are always toasted and have not been hulled. This gives them a rich, nutty flavor and a texture that pops when you bite into them, and they're typically white, black or gold in color. Hulled and untoasted sesame seeds are used in other ethnic cuisines, so look for sesame seeds in Asian grocery stores that are plump, with a matte surface.

Shirataki noodles (しらたき) *Shirataki* literally means "white waterfall" in Japanese, referring to the appearance of the long white noodles. Shirataki are made from glucomannin, extracted from the root of the konjac plant. The noodles have a firm, gelatinous texture that sets them apart from wheat-flour noodles. Composed almost entirely of water, they contain almost no calories.

Variations on these noodles are available in the refrigerated section of most supermarkets, thanks to the recent popularity of gluten-free and low-carb diets. Look out for Tofu Shirataki from the House Foods brand in the United States and Dry Konjac Shirataki Noodles from Zen Pasta in Europe.

Soy sauce (醤油) Although soy sauce is a condiment used throughout most of Asia, each country has its own distinct take on this seasoning. Different ratios of the base ingredients, as well as varying fermentation and aging times, give each version a completely different texture, taste and fragrance. Unless otherwise specified, we recommend using only Japanese soy sauce (*shoyu*) for the recipes in this book. Substituting other types of soy sauce can affect their flavor and saltiness.

Although regular Japanese soy sauce is used in this book, it is worth noting that within Japan there are different types of soy sauce, including *koikuchi* (regular dark soy sauce), *usukuchi* (light color and saltier) and *shiro* (literally, "white," a paler soy sauce that does not change the color of the food and is often used by high-end restaurants for this reason).

Because Japanese soy sauce is made from soybeans and wheat, it is not gluten-free. If you are following a gluten-free diet, you can use tamari as an alternative. Tamari is typically made with just soybeans and salt (but do always check the label). Be aware, however, that tamari has a stronger flavor and a darker color than regular soy sauce, so you will most likely have to reduce the quantity stated in the recipe and adjust the seasoning with salt.

BASIC
RECIPES

Basic Recipes

Making bento lunches a regular part of your routine is all about finding shortcuts. The recipes in this section include sauces that can be made in advance, as well as basic recipes that are used throughout this book.

Basic White Rice

Japanese rice is stickier than other types of rice, making it easy to eat with chopsticks from a bento box. Other types of rice do not work well as part of a bento. The easiest way to make rice is with an electric rice cooker. If you don't have one, here are stovetop directions. These instructions are for a gas or induction cooktop. Because electric coil and plate type radiant cooktops retain heat, I do not recommend using them for making rice. One rice-cooker cup of uncooked rice is roughly equivalent to three-quarters of a US cup, which makes two servings of rice.

FOR 2 SERVINGS
PREPARATION TIME 1 HOUR

³/4 cup (150 g) uncooked Japanese short-grain rice
1 cup (240 ml) cold water

Put the rice in a strainer and rinse under cold water, using your hand to agitate the grains until the water runs clear.

Dump the drained rice into a deep pot, add the water and cover with a lid. Let the rice soak for at least 30 minutes before you start cooking it.

Keeping the pot covered, turn the heat to high and bring the water to a boil. Once the water boils, turn the heat down to low and set the timer for 12 minutes. If it starts to boil over, temporarily remove from the heat until the contents settle, but do not open the lid.

When the timer goes off, turn off the heat and let the rice steam for another 15 minutes without opening the lid.

Fluff the rice with a spatula and allow it to cool to room temperature before packing it into your bento box.

Basic Brown Rice

Brown rice is rice that has not had the fibrous bran and nutrient-rich germ milled off. It's higher in fiber and protein than white rice; however, it takes a little longer to cook, and isn't as sticky as white rice. To make the rice sticky enough to hold together in dishes such as onigiri rice balls, I add some extra water, and I always let the rice soak for at least 30 minutes before cooking.

FOR 2 SERVINGS
PREPARATION TIME 1 HOUR 15 MINUTES

3/4 cup (150 g) uncooked Japanese short-grain brown rice
1 1/2 cups (360 ml) cold water

Put the rice in a strainer and rinse under cold water, using your hand to agitate the grains until the water runs clear.

Dump the drained rice into a deep pot, add the water and cover with a lid. Let the rice soak for at least 30 minutes before you start cooking it.

Keeping the pot covered, turn the heat to high and bring the water to a boil. Once the water boils, turn the heat down to low and set the timer for 30 minutes. If it starts to boil over, temporarily remove the pot from the heat until the contents settle, but do not open the lid.

When the timer goes off, turn off the heat and let the rice steam for another 15 minutes without opening the lid.

Fluff the rice with a spatula and let it cool to room temperature before packing into your bento box.

Sushi Rice

Sushi rice is cooked white Japanese rice that has been seasoned with sugar, salt and rice vinegar. Rice that is going to be mixed with sushi vinegar should be cooked with less water so it does not get mushy. For this reason, it's also important to cool the rice rapidly so that any excess liquid can evaporate before it soaks into the rice. The easiest way to do this is to point an electric fan at your rice as you fold in the sushi vinegar, but you can also have someone fan the rice by hand as you work.

FOR 2 SERVINGS
PREPARATION TIME 1 HOUR 15 MINUTES

3/4 cups (150 g) uncooked Japanese short-grain rice
3/4 cup + 2 tablespoons (210 ml) water
3 tablespoons Sushi Vinegar (see page 38)

Cook the rice as directed in the Basic White Rice recipe (see facing page), but using the proportion of rice to water in this recipe.

As soon as the rice is done steaming, dump it out into a large bowl and pour the sushi vinegar evenly over it.

Use a fan to cool the rice as you incorporate the sushi vinegar by folding it in with a rice paddle or spatula. The idea is to coat each grain of rice with the mixture, without breaking or mashing the grains.

The rice is ready when the sushi vinegar has been evenly incorporated, and the rice has cooled to lukewarm.

Sushi Vinegar

This versatile condiment is used to season sushi rice, but it's also great for dressing salads, marinating fish and making quick pickles. It will keep in the refrigerator for months. I like to make a big batch and store it in a bottle so that it's always ready to add a splash of flavor to my favorite bento side dishes.

MAKES ½ CUP (120 ML)
PREPARATION TIME 15 MINUTES

½ cup (120 ml) rice vinegar
6 tablespoons granulated sugar
2 teaspoons salt

Add all ingredients to a non-reactive pan over medium heat and whisk until the sugar and salt are dissolved. Do not allow the mixture to boil.

Let the sushi vinegar cool completely before transferring to a bottle and storing in the refrigerator.

3S Sauce

Named after the three ingredients that go into it, 3S sauce is used extensively throughout this book. It can be used as a marinade for meat or fish; when boiled until the sugar starts to caramelize, it becomes teriyaki sauce. As long as you store it in a sterile container, it will keep in the fridge for months. I recommend making a large batch so you always have some on hand.

MAKES 1 CUP (240 ML)
PREPARATION TIME 15 MINS

½ cup (100 g) granulated sugar
½ cup (120 ml) soy sauce
½ cup (120 ml) sake

1 Add all ingredients to a clean pot over medium heat and whisk together until the sugar is fully dissolved.

2 Let the sauce cool to room temperature and store it in a clean bottle in the refrigerator.

Tonkatsu Sauce

Tonkatsu Sauce is a sweet and savory sauce that's used as both a seasoning and condiment. Although it's most commonly used as a sauce for its namesake dish *tonkatsu* (deep-fried pork cutlets), this sauce can also be used to season stir-fries, to flavor sauces and even to dress salads. Tonkatsu sauce is traditionally made from a wide variety of vegetables, fruits and spices, but you can make a close approximation using just a handful of common ingredients.

MAKES 1 CUP (240 ML)
PREPARATION TIME 10 MINUTES

½ cup (120 ml) Worcestershire sauce
¼ cup (60 ml) honey
¼ cup (60 ml) ketchup
2 tablespoons soy sauce

1 Add all ingredients to a pot over medium-high heat and bring the sauce to a boil, stirring continuously.

2 Let the sauce cool to room temperature, then transfer to a clean bottle. Store in the refrigerator until ready to use.

Infused Basil Oil

Similar to Italian pesto, this vibrant green herb oil is the perfect addition to dressings and stir-fries for a rapid shot of flavor and color. We've called for basil here, but it can easily be made with other herbs such as shiso, thyme or sage. It will keep for weeks in a sealed container in the refrigerator. Due to the relatively small amount of liquid, most full-sized blenders will have difficulty spinning all the ingredients together, which is why we recommend using a hand blender. You could also use a small food processor, or double the recipe to make the sauce in a full-sized blender or food processor.

MAKES ¾ CUP (180 ML)
PREPARATION TIME 5 MINUTES

¾ cup (180 ml) olive oil
2 sprigs fresh basil
½ teaspoon salt

Combine all the ingredients in a round container with steep sides just wide enough to fit your hand blender. Blend together until it forms a smooth green oil.

Edible Decorations

Decorations are a great way to liven up your bento. In this section, Maki's going to show you how to turn simple ingredients like cheese, quail eggs and potatoes into all kinds of fun shapes. You can find quail eggs at high-end groceries. They have a high ratio of yolk to white, so they can be molded more easily than regular eggs without cracking.

Cheese Pandas

MAKES 2 PANDAS
PREPARATION TIME 5 MINUTES

1 slice American cheese
1 small nori sheet

1 Fold the cheese slice in half, doubling its thickness (picture 1).

2 With a small heart-shaped vegetable or cookie cutter cut two hearts out of the cheese (picture 2).

3 With small scissors cut 2 thin triangles from the nori (picture 3).

4 Use a nori punch or the scissors to cut two very small ovals and 12 small ovals out of the nori (picture 3).

5 Place the nori triangles in the center of each heart (picture 4).

6 Place a very small oval of nori to form the nose of each panda.

7 Arrange the rest of the nori to make the ears, eyes, feet and one hand for each panda.

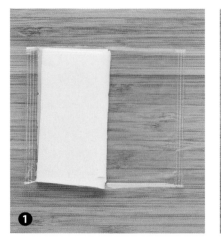

Cheese Butterflies

MAKES 2 BUTTERFLIES
PREPARATION TIME 2 MINUTES

1 slice American cheese
1 green bean, blanched

1 Fold the cheese slice in half, doubling its thickness (picture 1).

2 Use a flower-shaped vegetable or cookie cutter with five round petals to cut two flowers out of the cheese (picture 2).

3 Use the round part of a cookie cutter or a large straw to cut a semicircle into one of the petals (picture 3).

4 Cut a ¾-inch (2 cm) long piece from the green bean. Slice it in half lengthwise (pictures 4 and 5).

5 Cut a slit two-thirds of the way down each piece of green bean to make the body and antennae of each butterfly. Place onto the cheese as shown in picture 6.

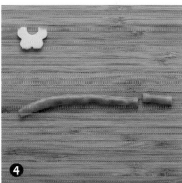

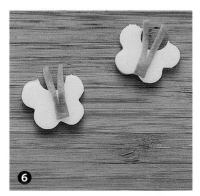

Potato Snowflakes

MAKES 4 SNOWFLAKES
PREPARATION TIME 7 MINUTES

1 baby potato

1 Peel the potato and cut the round ends off. Slice into ¼-inch (6 mm) thick slices and boil until just tender (picture 1).

2 Use a flower-shaped cookie cutter with sharp corners, such as this daffodil-shaped one, to cut each slice of potato into a flower shape (pictures 2 and 3).

3 Use a corner of the cutter to cut notches into the petals to form snowflakes as shown (pictures 4 and 5).

Potato Stars

MAKES 4 TO 5 STARS
PREPARATION TIME 7 MINUTES

1 baby potato
1 small nori sheet

1 Peel the potato and cut the round ends off. Slice into ¼-inch (6 mm) thick slices and boil until just tender (picture 1).

2 Use a small star-shaped vegetable or cookie cutter to cut each slice of potato into a star (picture 2).

3 Cut eyes and mouths out of the nori with a nori punch or small scissors (picture 3).

4 Use tweezers or a toothpick to place the eyes and mouth on each star (pictures 4 and 5).

Small Egg Spheres

MAKES 4 SPHERES
PREPARATION TIME 7 MINUTES

4 quail eggs

1 Bring a pot of water to a rolling boil. Use a spoon or ladle to gently lower the quail eggs into the boiling water.
2 Boil the eggs for 3 minutes.
3 Drain the eggs and peel them as soon as they have cooled enough to touch (picture 1) as they need to be hot for the next step to work. If you plan on dyeing the eggs, be sure to fully remove the membrane between the shell and the egg white or they will not dye evenly.
4 Squeeze each peeled egg between your fingers to shape into a sphere (picture 2). Dye after shaping.

Small Egg Flowers

MAKES 4 FLOWERS
PREPARATION TIME 8 MINUTES

4 quail eggs
1 cup (240 ml) water
1/2 teaspoon turmeric powder

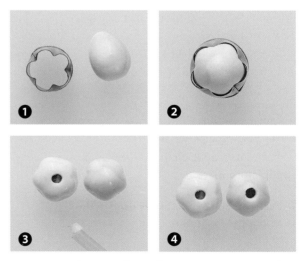

1 Bring a pot of water to a rolling boil. Use a spoon or ladle to gently lower the quail eggs into the boiling water. Boil the eggs for 3 minutes.
2 Drain the eggs and rinse in cold water until cool enough to peel. Be sure to fully remove the membrane between the shell and the egg white, or they will not dye evenly.
3 In a very small saucepan, bring the water and turmeric powder to a boil. Add the peeled quail eggs and cook until they've reached the desired shade of yellow. If the eggs aren't completely submerged in the liquid, be sure to turn them over regularly so that they are dyed evenly.
4 Remove the eggs from the turmeric water and press them into small flower-shaped cutters until they hold their shape (pictures 1 and 2).
5 With a straw, cut a round hole in the white at the center of each flower to expose the egg yolk. (pictures 3 and 4).

Small Egg Chicks

MAKES 4 CHICKS
PREPARATION TIME 5 MINUTES

1 cup (240 ml) water
½ teaspoon turmeric powder
4 Small Egg Spheres (see facing page)
2 thin slices carrot, boiled until tender
1 small nori sheet

1 In a very small saucepan, bring the water and turmeric powder to a boil.

2 Add the quail egg spheres and cook until they've reached the desired shade of yellow (picture 1). If the eggs aren't completely submerged in the liquid, be sure to turn them over regularly so that they dye evenly.

3 Use a straw pinched between your fingers to cut oval beaks out of the sliced carrot (picture 2).

4 Use a nori punch or small scissors to cut eyes out of the nori (picture 3).

5 Use tweezers to place the carrot beak and nori eyes on each dyed quail egg (picture 4).

You can see Small Egg Chicks used in the Fried Egg and Chicken Meatball Bento on page 52.

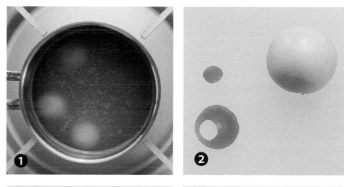

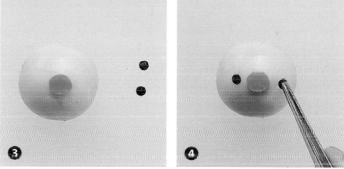

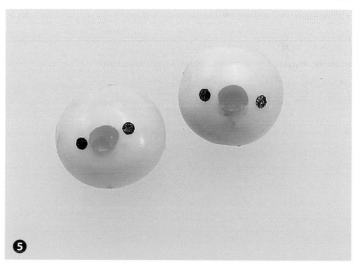

Small Egg Rabbits

MAKES 4 RABBITS
PREPARATION TIME 3 MINUTES

4 Smalll Egg Spheres (see page 44)
8 slices blanched almonds
1 small nori sheet

1 Cut a slit halfway through the middle of each quail egg sphere (picture 1).

2 Insert two slices of almond into the slits in the eggs as shown to make rabbit ears (picture 2).

3 Use a nori punch or small scissors to cut out eyes, noses and mouths for the rabbits from the nori (picture 3).

4 Use tweezers or a toothpick to place the facial features onto each rabbit (picture 4).

Small Egg Sea Turtles

MAKES 2 TURTLES
PREPARATION TIME 8 MINUTES

2 quail eggs
Soy sauce, for soaking
1 slice American cheese

1 Bring a pot of water to a rolling boil. Use a spoon or ladle to gently lower the quail eggs into the boiling water.

2 Boil the eggs for 3 minutes.

3 Drain the eggs and peel them as soon as they have cooled enough to touch. If you want the turtle shells to have a marbled appearance, leave some of the membrane between the shell and the egg white on the egg (picture 1).

4 Put the eggs in a small container and cover with soy sauce. Allow to sit until they reach the desired color (picture 2).

5 Fold the sliced cheese in half, doubling its thickness (picture 3).

6 Use a toothpick held at a 45-degree angle to cut 4 large flippers, 4 small flippers, and two heads out of the cheese. Arrange the head and flippers on a surface (picture 4).

7 Place the dyed quail egg on the cheese with the wide end toward the head (picture 5).

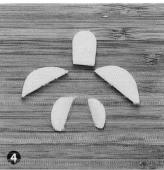

Apple Rabbits

MAKES 4 RABBITS
PREPARATION TIME 10 MINUTES

¹/₄ apple
¹/₂ lemon

1 Cut and core the apple as shown in pictures 1 to 5 to make 2 thin wedges.

2 Slice each wedge in half crosswise (picture 6).

3 Cut a V-shaped slit into the skin on the broad end of each piece (pictures 7 and 8).

4 Slide your knife under the skin of each piece just past the tip of the "v." Remove the triangle of skin (picture 9).

5 Continue sliding your knife under the skin until the skin is separated from two-thirds of each piece of apple (picture 10).

6 Squeeze lemon juice on the cut surfaces (picture 11).

7 Drop the apple rabbits into a bowl of water with some lemon juice squeezed into it. Soak until the tips of the rabbits' ears begin to curl upward (picture 12).

See an Apple Rabbit used in the Hamburger Cutlet Bento on page 64.

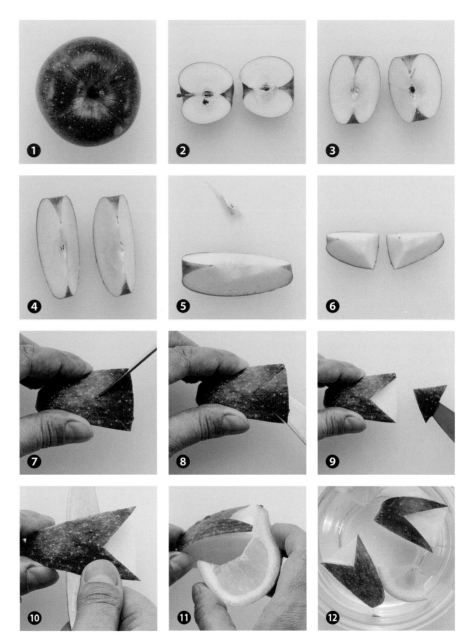

Sausage Octopuses

MAKES 4 OCTOPUSES
PREPARATION TIME 5 MINUTES

2 cocktail sausages
1 slice American cheese
1 small nori sheet

1 Halve each sausage at a 45° angle (picture 1).

2 Cut 4 slits into the tip of each piece of sausage (picture 2). Drop the sausages into boiling water and cook until the slits start to curl (picture 3).

3 For the mouths, use a regular straw to cut 4 circles of cheese (picture 4). Use a small straw to cut the center from each cheese circle to make a ring. Use tweezers to place a ring of cheese onto each sausage as shown (picture 5).

4 Cut eyes for the octopuses with a nori punch or small scissors. Position the eyes using tweezers (picture 6).

See Sausage Octopuses in the Chicken and Egg Soboro Bento on page 148.

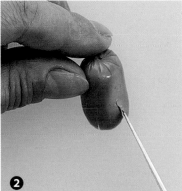

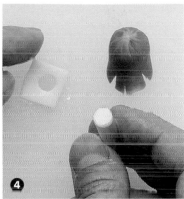

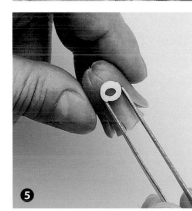

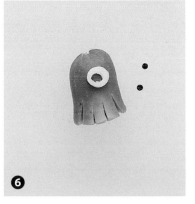

THE
RECIPES

Fried Egg and Chicken Meatball Bento | Maki

Do you like chicken teriyaki? How about fried eggs? If so, you're going to love these tasty teriyaki style fried eggs, paired with the Japanese-style chicken meatballs that are called *tsukune* in Japan.

Teriyaki sauce is delicious, of course, but did you know that it's also versatile and easy to put together? Made with equal parts soy sauce, sugar and sake, it goes with almost anything, including odds and ends from the fridge. It's a magical sauce that can turn even the most basic ingredients into a bento-worthy side dish.

One morning, my son came up to me and said, "Mom, I need a bento today." Unprepared and a little panicked, I raided the fridge and found a couple of eggs and some 3S sauce, which is how the Teriyaki Eggs recipe was born.

Teriyaki reminds me of chicken tsukune, so I added some of these savory meatballs to round out the bento. The juices from the chicken tsukune and the teriyaki sauce season the rice, making every last bite mouthwatering!

Cabbage Mushroom Corn Stir-fry

FOR 2 BENTOS
PREPARATION TIME 5 MINUTES

1 teaspoon butter
1 large cabbage leaf, about 2 oz (50 g), cut into 1/2-inch (1 cm) strips
Handful shimeji mushrooms, or mushrooms of your choice
2 tablespoons canned corn kernels
Salt, to taste
Black pepper, to taste

1 Melt the butter in a pan over medium low heat. Sauté the cabbage, corn and mushrooms until the cabbage is tender. Season with salt and pepper to taste.

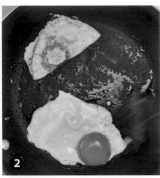
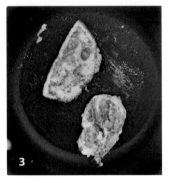
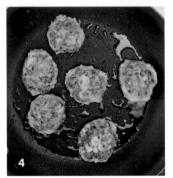

Chicken Meatballs and Teriyaki Eggs

FOR 2 BENTOS
PREPARATION TIME 10 MINUTES

FOR THE CHICKEN MEATBALLS

4 oz (120 g) ground chicken
1/2 small onion, about 2 oz (50 g), finely chopped
2 tablespoons all-purpose flour
1/2 beaten egg
Salt, to taste
1/2 teaspoon grated ginger

FOR THE TERIYAKI EGGS

Vegetable oil, for frying
2 eggs
All-purpose flour, for dusting
3 tablespoons 3S Sauce (see page 38)

1 Mix the Chicken Meatball ingredients in a bowl and knead well by hand. Shape the mixture into four to six patties, according to the size of your bento box.

2 Heat the oil in a nonstick frying pan over medium-low heat. Break the eggs into it, keeping them on opposite sides of the pan (pictures 1 and 2). Once the egg white is mostly cooked through, fold each egg in half with a spatula (picture 3). When fully cooked, remove them from the pan.

3 Fry the chicken patties until golden brown on each side (picture 4).

4 Return the eggs to the pan. With a sieve, dust both sides of the eggs and meatballs with flour (picture 5).

5 Add the 3S Sauce and cook over medium-high heat until it caramelizes (picture 6).

How to pack the bento

Spread the rice lengthwise across half of the box. Create a partition with leaves. Pack the Chicken Meatballs and Teriyaki Eggs next to the leaves. Place another leaf behind the Teriyaki Eggs and pack the Cabbage Mushroom Corn Stir-fry in the new space. Garnish with cherry tomatoes and Small Egg Chicks (see page 45).

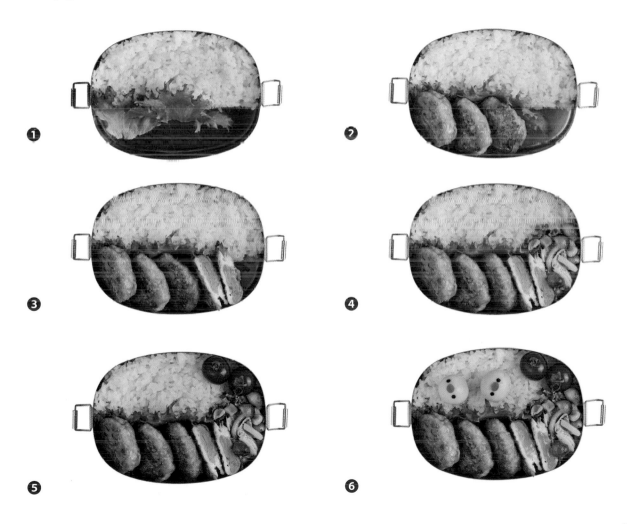

Loco Moco Hamburg Steak Bento | Marc

I love Loco Moco because it pulls together influences from around the world in a delicious, comforting dish that could only have been invented in Hawaii. I didn't grow up eating it, but it would have fit right in at my family's table.

In its purest traditional form, Loco Moco is a plain hamburger patty served over rice, smothered in brown gravy and topped with an egg. For my take on this recipe, I like to use a Japanese-style hamburg steak; this not only makes the dish more flavorful, but adding panko breadcrumbs and milk helps keep the patty tender even after it's cooled off. As for the egg, Loco Moco is usually served with a sunny-side up-egg, but putting a partially cooked egg into a bento box is a food safety risk, so I pack this with a hard-boiled egg instead.

Macaroni Salad

FOR 2 BENTOS
PREPARATION TIME 20 MINUTES

¼ cup (30 g) dry macaroni
2 small slices carrot, cut into matchsticks
½ cup (120 ml) milk
⅛ teaspoon salt
1 tablespoon mayonnaise
1 teaspoon Sushi Vinegar (see page 38)
1 slice ham, chopped
2-inch (5 cm) length celery, diced
1 leaf of a green onion (scallion), finely chopped
Black pepper, to taste

1 Combine the macaroni, carrots, milk and salt in a small saucepan. Bring to a bare simmer and cook until the pasta is very tender and there is only a little liquid left.

2 Let the macaroni cool, and then stir in the mayonnaise, Sushi Vinegar, ham, celery and green onions. Season with black pepper to taste.

Loco Moco Hamburg Steak

FOR 2 TO 3 BENTOS
PREPARATION TIME 20 MINUTES

FOR THE HAMBURG STEAK
½ small onion, about 2 oz (50 g), finely
  minced
¼ cup (15 g) panko breadcrumbs
2 tablespoons milk
2 teaspoons oyster sauce
¼ teaspoon black pepper
8 oz (225 g) ground beef
2 teaspoons vegetable oil

FOR THE GRAVY
½ cup (120 ml) low-sodium beef stock
1 tablespoon soy sauce
2 teaspoons potato starch
½ teaspoon Worcestershire sauce
5 small button mushrooms, sliced
½ small onion, about 2 oz (50 g), finely
  minced
1 tablespoon cream

FOR SERVING
1 hard-boiled egg, peeled and halved

1 Place the minced onion for the Hamburg steak in a small microwave-safe bowl. Cover with plastic wrap and microwave for 4 minutes at 800 watts. Let cool enough to handle.

2 Meanwhile, combine the panko, milk, oyster sauce and black pepper in a bowl and stir to mix.

3 Add the cooled onions and the ground beef to the panko mixture. Knead together by hand until is uniform in color.

4 Divide the meat mixture into 4 equal portions. Shape each portion into a thin oval patty about ¾-inch (2 cm) thick.

5 Heat the vegetable oil in a nonstick frying pan over medium heat and add the patties. Fry until well browned on one side, and then flip and brown the other side.

6 In the meantime, mix the beef stock, soy sauce, potato starch and Worcestershire sauce for the gravy together in a bowl.

7 Remove the browned patties from the pan and add the mushrooms and onions for the gravy. Sauté until the onions are tender and the mushrooms start to brown.

8 Return the patties to the pan. Give the beef stock mixture a quick stir to ensure the starch is dissolved, and add it to the pan. Once the sauce thickens, add the cream and turn off the heat.

How to pack the bento

Spread a layer of rice across two thirds of the bento box, leaving a little space at the top left corner. Place the patties and sauce in the open space to the right of the rice. Add half of a boiled egg next to the patties and fill any gaps with lettuce. Pack the Macaroni Salad into the top left corner, using a piece of lettuce to separate it from the rice. Place a few slices of pineapple on top of the rice.

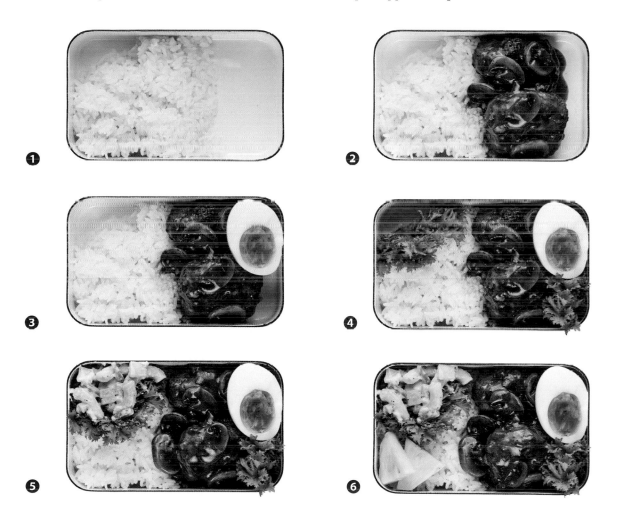

Karaage Fried Chicken Bento | Maki

When my son was ten years old, he wrote an essay entitled "My Favorite Thing." He later gave a presentation about it in front of his class during an open house. I'll never forget what he said: "Mom's karaage fried chicken is the best in the world!" Wow!

He was a picky eater, so it was a struggle preparing meals for him. At that time, he would eat only a few kinds of vegetables, meat and fish, but karaage was always a sure bet. I wonder how many times I made it for him!

Karaage, a staple of home cooking in Japan, is one of the most popular bento items because it's delicious at room temperature. Every household has its own variation, but the recipe I'm sharing here is a classic that's sure to be a hit with even the pickiest eater. I hope you enjoy it!

Karaage Fried Chicken

FOR 2 TO 3 BENTOS
PREPARATION TIME 10 MINUTES
MARINATING TIME 6 TO 8 HOURS

1 tablespoon soy sauce
1 teaspoon grated ginger
1 teaspoon grated garlic
2 to 3 skin-on chicken thighs, about
  7 oz (200 g) total, trimmed and cut
  into bite-sized pieces
Potato starch, for dusting
Vegetable oil, for deep-frying

1 In a zipper bag, combine the soy sauce, grated ginger and garlic. Add the chicken, massage to coat evenly and allow to marinate overnight.
2 Remove the marinated chicken from the bag. Coat each piece evenly with potato starch.
3 Heat the oil to 340°F (170°C) and fry the chicken for 4 to 5 minutes or until golden brown and cooked through.

Sautéed Zucchini

FOR 2 TO 3 BENTOS
PREPARATION TIME 10 MINUTES

½ zucchini
¼ teaspoon salt, plus more to taste
1 tablespoon all-purpose flour
1 teaspoon butter
Black pepper, to taste
1 teaspoon chopped parsley

1 Use a peeler to peel a striped pattern in the zucchini.

2 Slice the zucchini into ½-inch (1 cm) thick rounds. Sprinkle with the ¼ teaspoon salt and set aside for ten minutes.

3 Pat the zucchini dry with paper towels and then dust the slices evenly with the flour.

4 Melt the butter in a nonstick frying pan over medium heat and fry the zucchini until golden brown. When the zucchini is cooked, season with additional salt, pepper and chopped parsley to taste.

Pasta Salad

FOR 3 BENTOS
PREPARATION TIME 15 MINUTES

Small handful dry rotini pasta
1 small white potato, about 2 oz (50 g), peeled and chopped
1-inch (2.5 cm) piece Japanese or Persian cucumber, sliced thinly
¼ teaspoon salt, plus more to taste
1 tablespoon canned corn kernels
1 teaspoon canned tuna, drained
½ boiled egg
2 teaspoons mayonnaise
Black pepper, to taste

1 Cook the rotini according to the package directions.

2 Boil the potato until tender. Drain and mash.

3 Sprinkle the cucumber with the ¼ teaspoon salt and let rest for a few minutes to sweat. Squeeze between your hands to remove excess moisture.

4 Combine all ingredients in a bowl and stir together. Season with additional salt and pepper to taste.

How to pack the bento

Spread a portion of rice evenly across two-thirds of the bento box and add a salad leaf as a partition. Arrange the Karaage Fried Chicken on top of the leaves. Using a leaf to act as a partition, pack the Pasta Salad in front of the chicken. Arrange the Sautéed Zucchini and cherry tomatoes next to the Pasta Salad.

Hamburger Cutlet Bento | Maki

This seasoned hamburger patty, breaded in a crisp coating of panko breadcrumbs and then fried, is a hybrid of Hamburg steak and *tonkatsu*. It's called *menchi katsu* in Japanese: *menchi* is the Japanese transliteration of "minced," and *katsu* is the Japanese abbreviation for "cutlet." With a crisp exterior and tender center, it is a popular comfort food at the dinner table, and has become a classic bento item.

As with the Hamburg steak, every family has its own take on the hamburger cutlet, with different mixtures of meat, aromatics and sauces. This version has a piece of cheese inside that melts as the cutlet is fried. Crisp on the outside, with melted cheese on the inside, it's a wonderful complement to the rice. In our house we eat hamburger cutlets with commercial tonkatsu sauce, but if you can't find any, a recipe for a simple version of this classic sauce is on page 39.

Hamburger Cutlet

FOR 2 BENTOS
PREPARATION TIME 20 MINUTES

1 tablespoon panko breadcrumbs, plus more for breading
1 tablespoon milk
3½ oz (100 g) ground beef
½ small onion, about 2 oz (50 g), finely chopped
Salt, to taste
Black pepper, to taste
1 slice American cheese
2 tablespoons all-purpose flour
1 egg, beaten
Vegetable oil, for deep-frying
Tonkatsu Sauce, for serving (see page 39)

1 Soak the panko breadcrumbs in the milk.
2 Combine the beef, onion and soaked panko in a bowl and season with the salt and pepper.
3 Knead the mixture together thoroughly and shape into four balls of equal size.
4 Cut the sliced cheese into small pieces, divide into quarters, and tuck one quarter into the center of each meatball.
5 Form the meat into patties. Make a slight indentation into the center of each patty to make them cook through faster.
6 Dust each patty with flour. Dip each one in the egg and then bread each one evenly with the additional panko.
7 Heat the oil to 340°F (170°C). Deep-fry the cutlets until they are golden brown.

Japanese-style Coleslaw

FOR 2 BENTOS
PREPARATION TIME 15 MINUTES

½ small cabbage leaf, thinly sliced
2 thin slices carrot, julienned
1 thin slice daikon radish, julienned
½ teaspoon Sushi Vinegar
  (see page 38)
½ tablespoon canned corn kernels
½ slice ham, cut into thin strips
½ tablespoon mayonnaise
Salt, to taste
Black pepper, to taste

1 Combine the cabbage, carrot, daikon radish and Sushi Vinegar in a zipper bag and massage lightly. Let rest for ten minutes.

2 Squeeze out the excess liquid and transfer the vegetables to a bowl. Add the corn, ham and mayonnaise and stir to mix. Season with salt and pepper to taste.

How to pack the bento

Spread a portion of rice evenly across two-thirds of the bento box and add a leaf as a partition. Pack the Hamburger Cutlets next to the leaf. Place some Japanese-style Coleslaw in front of the cutlets. Put in another leaf as a partition next to the coleslaw and tuck some cherries and an Apple Rabbit (see page 48) into the remaining space.

❶

❷

❸

❹

Miso Salmon Bento | Marc

The modern Japanese diet contains dishes that were introduced to Japan at various points during its long history, but cured fish has been around for as long as humans have inhabited the Japanese archipelago. Fish cured with miso paste, known as *misozuke* in Japan, has only been around for about five hundred years, but it's most likely one of the original dishes served in bento boxes during the Edo period (1603-1868). While miso curing was originally to preserve food, the process makes the fish extremely flavorful. Fish prepared this way is the perfect accompaniment to a bento box packed with rice.

Though salmon is used here, this preparation is good with almost any fish that has a relatively high fat content, such as sablefish (black cod) and Patagonian toothfish (Chilean sea bass). It also works with other proteins such as chicken, pork or even tofu.

Broccolini in Sesame Oil
FOR 2 BENTOS
PREPARATION TIME 5 MINUTES

4 stalks broccolini or rapini
1 teaspoons toasted sesame oil
1/4 teaspoon soy sauce
Salt, to taste

1 Parboil the broccolini in boiling water for 30 seconds. Plunge into cold water to chill it rapidly.
2 Line the stems up and use your hands to squeeze as much water out of the broccolini as you can without tearing it apart.
3 Cut the greens into 2-inch (5 cm) lengths and toss in a bowl with the sesame oil and soy sauce. Add salt as needed.

Sesame Rice
FOR 2 BENTOS
PREPARATION TIME 30 MINUTES

2 servings Basic White Rice (see page 36)
1 tablespoon black sesame seeds

1 Follow the directions to make Basic White Rice.
2 When the rice is done steaming, add the black sesame seeds and fold the into the rice until the sesame seeds are evenly distributed.

Curing Proteins

Curing is the process of using salt to draw moisture out of food through osmosis. The lower water content, along with the higher salinity of the food, makes the environment inhospitable to microbes that cause food to spoil. This increases the shelf life of fresh food such as meat and fish, which is why humans have been curing food since antiquity.

Since most of us don't have time to go grocery shopping every day, curing is a great way to preserve proteins to use in a bento later in the week. Also, by reducing the water content, you're concentrating the flavors in the food, which makes dishes taste even better!

Although curing food will slow the growth of microbes, it will not stop the process, so it's essential to follow a few simple rules:

Be clean: Make sure all preparation surfaces and utensils are very clean, and use gloves when handling the food.

Fresh is best: Curing fish that's about to go bad won't make it any safer to eat. I usually cure food as soon as I bring it home from the store.

Keep it cold: Cured foods still need to be refrigerated.

Use your nose: If your cured food smells bad, throw it away.

Miso Salmon

FOR 2 BENTOS
PREPARATION TIME 10 MINUTES
CURING TIME 2 TO 3 DAYS

2 tablespoons yellow miso paste
2 tablespoons honey
1 tablespoon sake
1/2 teaspoon grated ginger
2 small fillets salmon, about 7 oz (200 g) total
1 teaspoon vegetable oil

1 Whisk the miso, honey, sake and ginger together in a small bowl until smooth (pictures 1 and 2).

2 Lay a large piece of plastic wrap on your work surface. Spread half of the miso marinade in an even layer in the center of the wrap (picture 3).

3 Lay the salmon fillets on the marinade layer (picture 4). Cover with the remaining marinade (picture 5.

4 Wrap the plastic wrap tightly around the salmon, squeezing out any air (picture 6). Let the salmon cure in the refrigerator for at least two days, or up to five days.

5 When you're ready to make your bento, use your hands to scrape off as much of the marinade as you can. Use a paper towel to remove any remaining marinade.

6 Heat a nonstick frying pan over medium heat. Add the oil and swirl it around.

7 Place the salmon in the pan and fry on one side until it's golden brown. Be careful, as the honey makes the salmon burn easily. If it gets too dark too quickly, turn down the heat.

8 Turn the salmon over and fry until the second side has browned and the salmon is cooked through.

How to cure the salmon

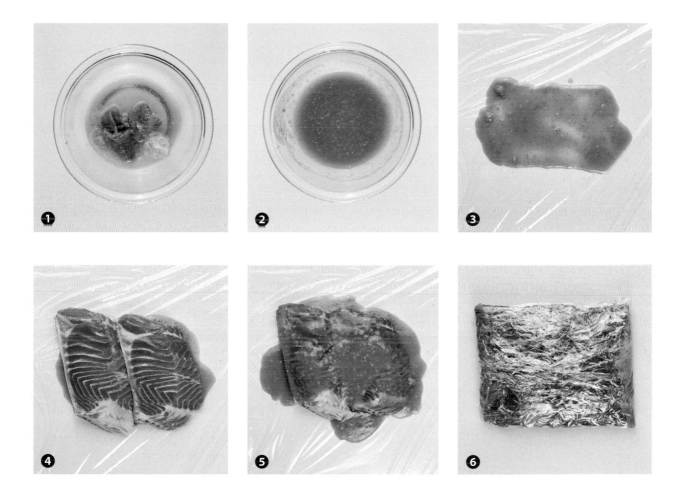

Taco Rice Bento | Marc

Tacos might not be the first thing to come to mind when you think of Okinawa, Japan's southernmost tropical island chain, but the longstanding US military presence there has influenced the local cuisine. Taco Rice has become an Okinawa specialty.

When I first heard of it, I imagined a taco-flavored rice pilaf. Many Japanese people wonder if it includes octopus (*tako* is Japanese for octopus). With seasoned ground beef and all the taco fixings layered on a pile of white rice, this dish is a mashup of Tex-Mex tacos and Japanese *donburi*.

Unlike its crisp-shelled parent, Taco Rice is perfect in a bento as it won't go soggy. If you don't want to forgo the shell, fear not! I always pack some tortilla chips separately to crumble on top. They also make a tasty scoop to get every bite into your mouth!

Taco Toppings
FOR 3 TO 4 BENTOS
PREPARATION TIME 15 MINUTES

2 tablespoons soy sauce
2 tablespoons sake
2 teaspoons ketchup
2 teaspoons vegetable oil
1/2 small onion, 2 1/2 oz (75 g), finely diced
1 large clove garlic, minced
2 teaspoons chili powder
1/4 teaspoon ground cumin
8 oz (225 g) ground beef
2 leaves iceberg lettuce, shredded
1 medium tomato, diced
Small handful grated cheese
Small handful cilantro leaves (for garnish)
Hot sauce, to taste (optional)
Tortilla chips, as desired

1 Prepare the sauce by whisking together the soy sauce, sake and ketchup.

2 Heat the oil in a nonstick frying pan over medium heat. Add the onion and garlic and sauté until tender and starting to brown.

3 Add the chili powder and cumin and continue sautéeing until fragrant.

4 Add the ground beef along with the sauce mixture. Working quickly, use the edge of a spatula to stir vigorously and break up the meat into small crumbs as it fries.

5 Continue frying the mixture until all of the liquid has evaporated. Transfer the beef mixture to a plate to cool.

6 See the packing instructions on page 75 for how to arrange the beef and the other toppings in the bento box.

Half-calorie Rice

FOR 3 TO 4 BENTOS
PREPARATION TIME 30 MINUTES

7 oz (200 g) shirataki noodles
³/4 cup (150 g) uncooked white rice
³/4 cup (180 ml) water

1 Chop the shirataki noodles into small pieces about the size of a grain of rice (pictures 1 and 2).

2 Put the rice in a strainer and rinse under cold water, using your hand to agitate the grains until the water runs clear.

3 Dump the drained rice into a deep pot along with the chopped shirataki and the water and cover with a lid. Turn the heat to high and bring the water to a boil. Once the water boils, turn the heat down to low and set a timer for 12 minutes. If the pot starts to boil over, temporarily remove the pot from the heat until the contents settle, but do not open the lid.

4 When the timer goes off, turn off the heat and let the rice steam for another 15 minutes without opening the lid.

5 Fluff the rice with a spatula and allow to cool to room temperature before packing it into your bento box.

How to pack the bento

Spread a portion of rice evenly across the bottom of the entire bento box and top with the meat, cheese, shredded lettuce, diced tomatoes and cilantro. Sprinkle on some more cheese. Pack the tortilla chips separately and crumble them on top of the bento just before eating.

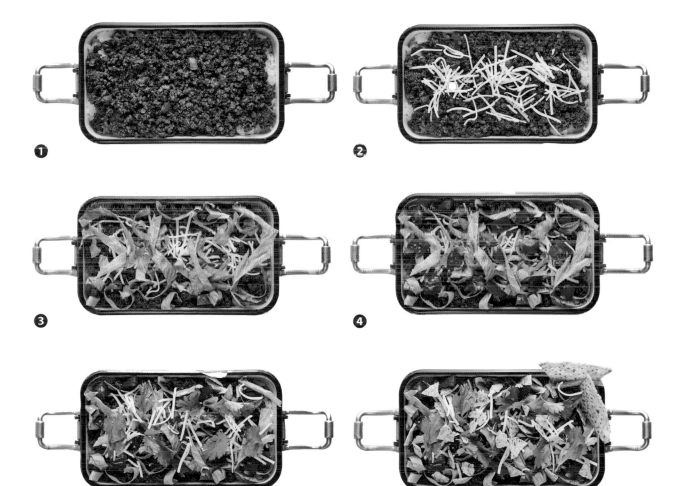

Yakitori Grilled Chicken Bento | Maki

Yaki means "grilled," and *tori* means "poultry," so *yakitori* is grilled poultry in Japanese. It's usually made by skewering pieces of chicken on bamboo skewers and then cooking them over an open charcoal grill. The grilled meat is typically seasoned with salt or a sweet and savory sauce.

For this bento, I've adapted some of these techniques so that the yakitori can be made at home with just a frying pan. The key is to salt the bite-sized pieces of chicken. This removes the excess water from the surface of the chicken, giving it a texture that's similar to chicken that's been prepared on a charcoal grill.

To finish it off, I like to glaze the chicken with a flavorful yakitori sauce that I make by adding honey to our 3S Sauce. If you enjoy spicy foods, try sprinkling the yakitori with some *shichimi togarashi* (Japanese seven-spice hot pepper seasoning).

Yakitori Grilled Chicken

FOR 3 BENTOS
PREPARATION TIME 15 MINUTES

2 skin-on chicken thighs, about 7 oz
  (200 g) total, trimmed
1/8 teaspoon salt
3 green onions (scallions), white
  part only
6 shishito peppers
2 tablespoons 3S Sauce (see
  page 38)
1 teaspoon honey

1 Cut the chicken into 10 to 12 bite-sized pieces. Sprinkle the meat with the salt and let it rest for 10 minutes.

2 Trim the green onions and poke holes in the peppers with a toothpick to prevent them from popping.

3 Dry the chicken with paper towels. Arrange the pieces skin-side down in a nonstick frying pan over medium-high heat.

4 Once some fat has rendered out from the chicken, add the green onions and peppers. Stir-fry until they are cooked through and the chicken is golden brown.

5 Transfer the chicken and vegetables to a plate and wipe the pan.

6 Add the 3S Sauce and honey to the pan and bring to a boil. When it starts to get thick, return the chicken and vegetables to the pan and glaze them with the sauce.

Sesame Asparagus

FOR 3 BENTOS
PREPARATION TIME 5 MINUTES

**2 to 3 stalks asparagus, cut into
  1-inch (2.5 cm) lengths (halve
  lengthwise if the spears are
  thick)**
1 teaspoon toasted sesame oil
Salt, to taste
Black pepper, to taste
Chicken bouillon powder, to taste
**¹/₂ teaspoon toasted white
  sesame seeds**

1 Blanch the asparagus for 1 to 2
minutes. Drain.
2 Combine the asparagus and
sesame oil in a bowl. Add the
salt, pepper and chicken bouillon.
Garnish with the sesame seeds.

How to pack the bento

Spread a portion of rice evenly across two-thirds of the bento box. Top the rice with Yakitori Grilled Chicken. Line the empty third of the box with leaves. Pack the Sesame Asparagus on top of the leaves. Partition off the asparagus using a leaf, and then tuck a few cherry tomatoes into the new space. Fill any remaining space with grapes.

Stuffed Bell Pepper Bento | Maki

Like most kids, I wasn't a fan of bell peppers growing up, as I didn't enjoy the bitter taste or the texture. When stuffed with meat, however, the peppers become tender and flavorful. This dish changed my mind about peppers.

In Japanese, we say *me de tanoshimu*, which means "to enjoy [food] with your eyes." The vibrant colors of mini-peppers make this dish far more beautiful than boring old brown meatballs, don't you think?

Peppers are rich in vitamins A, C and E. The best part is that these ripe peppers turn sweet when fried, which makes them the perfect compliment to the savory beef.

Sautéed Spinach and Mushrooms

FOR 2 BENTOS
PREPARATION TIME 5 MINUTES

2 teaspoons olive oil
2 cups (60 g) spinach, roughly chopped
4 button mushrooms, sliced
Salt, to taste
Black pepper, to taste

1 Heat the olive oil in a small frying pan.
2 Add the spinach and mushrooms and sauté until tender.
3 Season with salt and pepper to taste.

Stuffed Mini Bell Peppers

FOR 2 BENTOS
PREPARATION TIME 15 MINUTES

2 tablespoons panko breadcrumbs
1 tablespoon milk
3 oz (85 g) ground beef
1/2 small onion, about 2 1/2 oz (75 g),
  finely chopped
1 tablespoon all-purpose flour, plus more for
  dusting
1 teaspoon soy sauce
Salt, to taste
Black pepper, to taste
4 to 5 mini bell peppers, halved, seeds and
  stems removed
Vegetable oil, for pan-frying

1 Combine the panko and the milk in a bowl and allow to soak for a few minutes.

2 Add the beef, onion, 1 tablespoon of flour and the soy sauce. Season with salt and pepper and knead well to combine.

3 Dust the insides of the peppers with the additional flour (picture 1).

4 Stuff the peppers with the meat mixture (picture 2).

5 Heat the oil in a nonstick frying pan over medium-high heat and pan-fry the stuffed mini peppers until they are browned on both sides.

6 Turn the heat down to low and cover the pan with a lid. Let the peppers steam until the meat is cooked through.

How to pack the bento

Spread a portion of rice evenly across the bottom of the entire bento box. Place a salad leaf so that it spreads from the center third to the right third of the bento box, as shown in picture 2. Arrange some Stuffed Mini Bell Peppers in the larger space to the left of the leaf. Place a portion of Sautéed Spinach and Mushrooms behind the leaf.

Takikomi Tuna Rice Bento | Maki

Takikomi gohan, the Japanese version of rice pilaf, generally combines rice with mushrooms, vegetables and meat or seafood. It's a favorite in Japan, perhaps because making it is as simple as adding all of the ingredients to the pot when you cook the rice.

This dish is very flexible, and it's possible to come up with variations on the classic formula by substituting any of the ingredients. I like to change takikomi rice with the seasons. In spring, I add bamboo shoots; in summer, I add corn; in autumn, I add mushrooms; and in winter, I make my favorite — oyster rice!

For this version, I've simplified the recipe to use ingredients that are available year-round, including canned tuna, carrots, shimeji mushrooms and shirataki noodles. The rice gets its great flavor from the tuna, which eliminates the need to use dashi stock. The other ingredients are flexible and can be changed to suit your preferences.

Daikon and Carrot Pickles
FOR 2 TO 3 BENTOS
PREPARATION TIME 5 MINUTES
MARINATING TIME 6 TO 8 HOURS

1-inch (2.5 cm) length daikon radish, about 2 oz (50g), cut into matchsticks
1-inch (2.5 cm) length carrot, about 1 oz (30 g), cut into matchsticks
2 teaspoons Sushi Vinegar (see page 38)
Toasted white sesame seeds, for garnish

1 Combine the daikon, carrots and Sushi Vinegar in a zipper bag. Marinate overnight.
2 Drain the excess liquid and garnish with sesame seeds.

Takikomi Tuna Rice

FOR 2 BENTOS
PREPARATION TIME 35 MINUTES
SOAKING TIME 30 MINUTES

¾ cup (150 g) Japanese short-grain rice
1½ oz (40 g) shirataki noodles
¾ cup + 1 tablespoon (195 ml) water
2 teaspoons soy sauce
1 teaspoon sake
Salt, to taste
2 tablespoons canned tuna in oil
Handful shimeji mushrooms (or mushrooms of your choice), trimmed
¾-inch (2 cm) length carrot, about ¾ oz (20 g), cut into matchsticks
¾ oz (20 g) sliced canned bamboo shoots
1 green onion (scallion), chopped, for garnish

1 Rinse the rice until the water runs clear and then add it to a bowl with enough water to cover. Let stand for 30 minutes.

2 Parboil the shirataki noodles and drain well. Chop into small pieces.

3 Drain the rice. Transfer to a pot and add the water, soy sauce, sake, salt, tuna, mushrooms, carrot, bamboo and shirataki.

4 Cover the pot and bring to a boil over high heat. Reduce the heat to low and simmer for 15 minutes.

5 Turn off the heat and allow the rice to steam without opening the lid for 10 minutes.

6 When the rice is done steaming, fluff it with a spatula and allow to cool to room temperature, then garnish with the chopped green onion.

How to pack the bento

Line the inside of the basket with parchment paper and spread an even layer of Takikomi Tuna Rice into half of the basket. Place a leaf so that it partitions off the rice. Add the Daikon and Carrot Pickles on top of the leaf. Add more leaves to partition off the pickles and then tuck some fruit into the remaining space. If you plan to transport this bento, we recommend using a sealed container rather than a basket.

Chicken Nanban Bento | Marc

Although I grew up in the US, I was born in a small industrial town in southern Japan called Nobeoka. It's not known for much, but its culinary claim to fame is a tiny restaurant near the train station that is said to be the birthplace of Chicken Nanban.

This modern Japanese classic consisting of golden fried chicken soaked in a sweet and tangy sauce gets its name from *nanbanzuke*, which means something like "marinated European-style." It traces its roots back to a dish introduced to Japan by the Portuguese in the seventeenth century.

These days, most people make Chicken Nanban by simply dousing Chicken Karaage in the sauce, but the original recipe from my hometown was made with egg. Unlike flour or starch, the egg puffs up and crisps to form an airy coating that won't disintegrate. This makes it perfect for packing into a bento box for lunch.

Shredded Cabbage Salad

Cabbage might not be the first leafy green you think of for salad, but it's full of vitamin K, vitamin C, folate and fiber, as well as antioxidants and phytonutrients. All that fiber can make it a bit tough, but when it's thinly shredded it makes a delicious crisp salad.

FOR 2 BENTOS
PREPARATION TIME 10 MINUTES

2 leaves cabbage (about 5¹/2 oz or 150 g); use tender inner leaves
Cold water, for soaking

1 Remove the tough center stem from the cabbage and cut the leaves in half. Soak the leaves in cold water for at least 10 minutes to crisp them up.
2 Dry the leaves with paper towels and then stack and roll them up.
3 Slice the rolled cabbage as thinly as possible.

Chicken Nanban

FOR 2 BENTOS
PREPARATION TIME 10 MINUTES

FOR THE NANBAN SAUCE
3 tablespoons 3S Sauce (see page 38)
¼ teaspoon grated ginger
1 tablespoon rice vinegar

FOR THE CHICKEN
Vegetable oil, for frying
**2 to 3 skin-on chicken thighs, about 9 oz
  (250 g) total, cut into bite-sized pieces**
Salt
Black pepper
1 tablespoon all-purpose flour
1 egg, beaten

1 Combine the 3S Sauce and grated ginger in a small saucepan and bring to a boil. Keep boiling until the smell of alcohol is gone. Turn off the heat and stir in the rice vinegar.

2 Add 2 inches (5 cm) of oil to a heavy-bottomed pot and heat to 340°F (170°C).

3 Season the chicken with salt and pepper and dust with flour to coat evenly (picture 1).

4 When the oil is up to temperature, dip the chicken pieces in the beaten egg and then quickly lower them into the oil (pictures 2 and 3). Fry until the chicken is golden brown and cooked through.

5 Transfer the fried chicken straight into the pot with the Nanban Sauce and toss to coat evenly.

Tartar Sauce

FOR 2 BENTOS
PREPARATION TIME 2 MINUTES

1 hard-boiled egg, peeled and chopped
1 tablespoon finely diced celery
½ green onion (scallion), minced
2 tablespoons mayonnaise
½ teaspoon whole-grain mustard
Salt, to taste
Ground white pepper, to taste

1 Combine all ingredients in a bowl and stir gently to mix.

2 Adjust seasonings to taste as needed.

How to pack the bento

Fill one-third of the bento box to the top with rice, and spread a thinner layer of rice evenly across the remaining two-thirds of the box. Arrange Chicken Nanban pieces in the center third of the box. Tuck a serving of Shredded Cabbage Salad into the remaining third of the box on top of the thinner layer of rice. Decorate the Chicken Nanban with Tartar Sauce and garnish with tomato slices and snap peas.

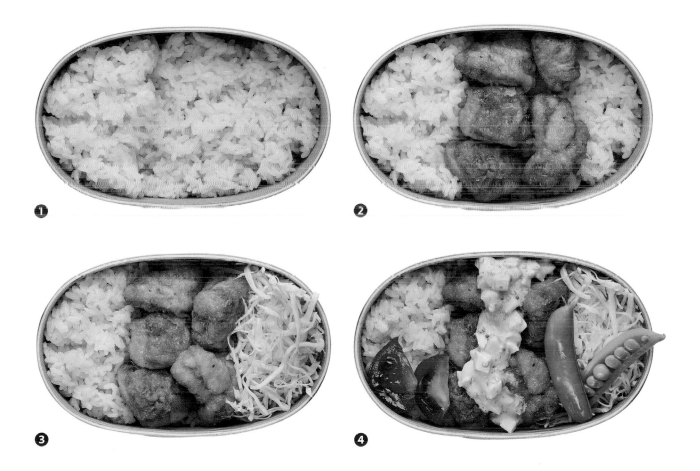

Summer Roll Bento | Marc

Vietnamese summer rolls are one of my favorite appetizers. Here, I've taken inspiration from Vietnamese summer rolls to create a satisfying two-course lunch menu that you can eat with your fingers. The first course features a Rainbow Salad Roll with a colorful medley of vegetables and herbs. The second course is a Char Siu Roll that packs all the components of a barbecued pork rice bowl into a rice-paper wrapper.

Cutting the rolls into bite-sized pieces not only makes them easier to eat, but it also exposes the vivid colors inside the wrapper. Each roll is individually seasoned, so they don't really need sauce, but dunking them on the way to your mouth is half the fun, so I've included a recipe for a creamy sesame dipping sauce.

Like all the recipes in this book, the components of this bento can be swapped into other bento menus or used to create something new. Cabbage and Carrot Pickles (below) is a refreshing, colorful side for any bento, and Char Siu Barbecued Pork (page 96) is sublime in a banh mi sandwich. Or how about stuffing some of the other dishes in this book into a Char Siu Roll (page 94)? Ginger Pork (page 104) or Chicken Nanban (page 90) are two items that would be amazing rolled into a rice-paper wrapper!

Cabbage and Carrot Pickles
FOR 4 RAINBOW SALAD ROLLS
PREPARATION TIME 20 MINUTES

1 leaf red cabbage, about 2 oz (50 g)
2-inch (5 cm) length carrot, about 2 oz
  (50 g) cut into thin matchsticks
2 tablespoons Sushi Vinegar (see page 38)
Pinch of salt

1 Trim the tough center stem from the cabbage and cut the leaf in half. Stack the cabbage, roll the layers together, and use a sharp knife to shred thinly.
2 Combine the cabbage, carrots and Sushi Vinegar in a bowl and allow to marinate for at least 15 minutes. (These quick pickles can be prepared up to a day in advance.)
3 Squeeze out excess liquid before using in the Rainbow Salad Rolls.

Char Siu Rolls and Rainbow Salad Rolls

FOR 3 TO 4 BENTO BOXES
PREPARATION TIME 10 MINUTES

8 rice-paper wrappers
Scant 1 cup (170 g) cooked Basic White Rice
  (see page 36)
8 leaves green shiso
1/2 Japanese or Persian cucumber, quartered
  lengthwise
20 chives, cut into 3 1/2-inch (9 cm) lengths
4 leaves lettuce
Cilantro, to taste
Cabbage and Carrot Pickles (see page 93)
Char Siu Barbecued Pork (see page 96)

1 Fill a plate or tray large enough to fit a
sheet of rice-paper wrapper with cold water.
Prepare a surface for rolling. Have all the
fillings prepped and ready.

2 Quickly dip one rice-paper wrapper in the
water to coat evenly and place on your prep
surface (pictures 1 and 2, facing page). It
should still be stiff at this point; if it's too wet
it will become mushy and likely to tear.

3 Lay 2 shiso leaves on the bottom third of the
wrapper (picture 3, facing page).

4 Spread a quarter of the pork over the shiso
leaves and then top with a quarter of the rice
(pictures 4 and 5, facing page).

5 Roll the bottom edge of the wrapper as
tightly over the filling as you can without
tearing the wrapper. Continue rolling to the
middle of the wrapper (picture 6, facing page).

6 Fold the two sides toward the center of
the roll and continue rolling up the rest of
the wrapper (pictures 7 and 8, facing page).
Repeat to make three more Char Siu Rolls.

7 For the Rainbow Salad Rolls, use the same
technique as for the Char Siu Rolls, layering
a quarter of the lettuce, Cabbage and Carrot
Pickles, cucumber, chives and cilantro inside
each roll (see pictures 1 to 4, below).

8 Use a wet knife to cut the rolls to fit your bento
box. I usually cut each roll into three pieces.

How to wrap the Rainbow Salad Rolls

How to wrap the Char Siu Rolls

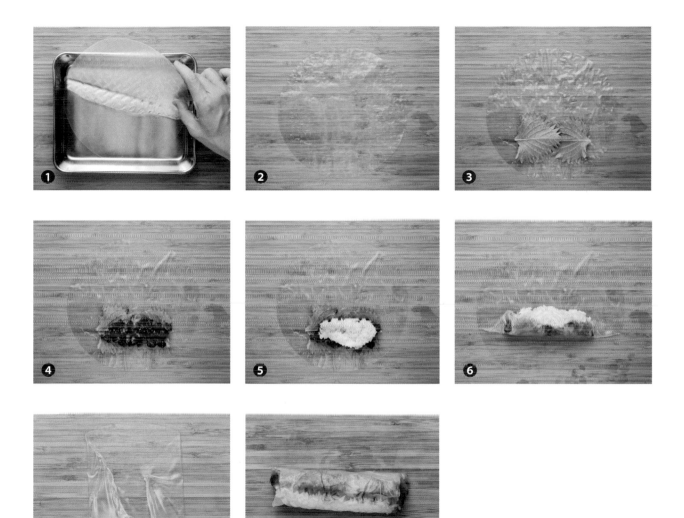

Sesame Sauce

FOR 4 CHAR SIU ROLLS
PREPARATION TIME 2 MINUTES

2 tablespoons tahini
2 teaspoons water
1¹/2 teaspoons soy sauce
1 teaspoon honey
¹/4 teaspoon toasted sesame oil

1 Combine all ingredients in a bowl and whisk together until smooth.

Char Siu Barbecued Pork

FOR 4 CHAR SIU ROLLS
PREPARATION TIME 20 MINUTES

4 teaspoons honey
2 teaspoons Shaoxing wine or sake
1 tablespoon Chinese dark soy sauce
1 small clove garlic, grated
¹/4 teaspoon five-spice powder
7 oz (200 g) pork belly, chopped into ¹/4-inch (6 mm) pieces

1 Whisk the honey, Shaoxing wine, soy sauce, garlic and five-spice powder together in a bowl. Add the pork and stir to coat evenly. Allow to marinate for at least 15 minutes. (Can be prepared up to a day in advance.)

2 To cook the meat, spread the marinated pork into a single layer in a cold nonstick frying pan.

3 Turn the heat to medium and cook without stirring until the liquid evaporates and some of the fat starts rendering out.

4 Stir-fry the pork until the sauce has caramelized into a shiny glaze around each piece of pork. Transfer to a plate and allow to cool completely before using in the Char Siu Rolls.

How to pack the bento

To pack the rolls into a two tier bento box, place a leaf at one end of each tier. Cut the Char Siu Rolls and Rainbow Salad Rolls to fit into the bento box and pack a few into each tier. Place leaves in front of the rolls to create a partition. Pack the sauce in a sealed container in one tier and tuck some fruit and vegetables into the space in the other tier.

Honey Lemon Chicken Bento | Marc

I grew up in a multi-ethnic household in Northern California, and our dinner table was often a reflection of the mixed makeup of our family. Despite running a business that had her working well into the night, my mom always made the time to prepare dinner so we could eat as a family.

This Honey Lemon Chicken was (and still is) one of my favorite meals. With juicy morsels of savory chicken enrobed in a lemony sauce that's brimming with umami, it's like the perfect mashup of barbecue and lemon chicken. For this bento, I've paired it with kabocha squash, its burst of orange color and nutty-sweet taste a perfect complement to the tangy chicken. If you can't find kabocha, you can use butternut or a similar sweet squash.

Kabocha Squash Rice

FOR 2 TO 3 BENTOS
PREPARATION TIME 30 MINUTES

³/₄ cup (150 g) uncooked Japanese short-
  grain rice
1 cup (240 ml) cold water
Thick slice kabocha squash, about
  3 oz (85 g), or other winter squash

1 Wash and drain rice following the Basic White Rice recipe on page 36.
2 Slice the squash into ¹/₃-inch (8 mm) thick pieces, and then cut the slices into squares. Add to the rice. Cook the rice following the instructions on page 36.

Honey Lemon Chicken

FOR 2 TO 3 BENTOS
PREPARATION TIME 10 MINUTES

FOR THE SAUCE

2 tablespoons white wine
1¹/2 tablespoons tomato paste
1¹/2 tablespoons honey
Grated zest from ¹/4 lemon
1 tablespoon lemon juice
1 teaspoon soy sauce

FOR THE CHICKEN

3 skin-on chicken thighs, about 10 oz
  (300 g) total, cut into bite-sized pieces
Salt, to taste
Black pepper, to taste
1 tablespoon all-purpose flour
1 tablespoon vegetable oil
1 clove garlic, minced

1 Whisk the wine, tomato paste, honey, lemon zest, lemon juice and soy sauce together in a bowl to make the sauce.

2 Season the chicken pieces on both sides with salt and pepper and then dust evenly with the flour.

3 Heat a nonstick frying pan over medium heat and add the oil, swirling to coat the pan.

4 Add the chicken, skin-side down, and let it brown on one side.

5 Flip the chicken over and scatter the garlic around the pan.

6 When the chicken has browned on the second side, use a paper towel to remove any excess oil from the pan.

7 Add the sauce and quickly cover with a lid. Allow the chicken to steam for 2 to 3 minutes, or until it's cooked through.

8 Remove the lid and toss to coat the chicken. Continue cooking until the sauce has formed a thick glaze.

Ginger Pork Bento | Maki

Buta no shogayaki, meaning ginger-grilled pork, is one of the most popular dishes in Japanese homes because it's so delicious and simple to make. Shogayaki (ginger-grilled) usually refers to pork, but the fragrant ginger sauce goes well with steak, chicken, salmon or even veggies.

For this bento, I use thinly sliced pork and marinate it in the sweet and savory sauce made with sake, soy sauce, sugar and — of course! — ginger. Aside from tasting amazing, ginger also has the power to tenderize meat, which helps keep the pork in the bento from getting tough, even at room temperature.

If the smell of ginger makes you as hungry as it does me, you're going to love this bento!

Potato Salad

FOR 2 TO 3 BENTOS
PREPARATION TIME 20 MINUTES

1/2 Japanese or Persian cucumber, thinly sliced
2 broccoli florets, cut into bite-sized pieces and
  blanched for 2 minutes
1 tablespoon canned corn kernels
2 small white potatoes, about 4 oz (120g), diced
  and boiled
1 slice ham, diced
1 tablespoon mayonnaise
Salt, to taste
Black pepper, to taste

1 Sprinkle the cucumbers with salt and let them rest for a few minutes to sweat. Squeeze out the excess liquid between your hands.
2 Combine the remaining ingredients in a bowl. Add the squeezed cucumber and adjust seasoning to taste.

Mini Bell Pepper Stir-fry

FOR 2 TO 3 BENTOS
PREPARATION TIME 10 MINUTES

1 teaspoon vegetable oil
4 to 5 mini bell peppers, trimmed, seeded
  and cut into thin strips
Soy sauce, to taste
Salt, to taste
Black pepper, to taste
Toasted white sesame seeds, to taste

1 Heat the vegetable oil in a nonstick frying pan over medium heat.
2 Add the bell peppers and sauté until tender.
3 Season with soy sauce, salt and pepper. Garnish with the sesame seeds.

The Power of Ginger

Most of us use ginger to season food because it tastes great, but did you know that this rhizome has other hidden powers? Since the meat in a bento is typically cold by the time it's consumed, making sure it's tender is essential. Ginger contains an enzyme called zingibain that breaks the peptide bonds in proteins that make meat tough; this makes it an effective meat tenderizer.

Ginger also contains compounds such as gingerol, paradol and zerumbone, which are all known to have antimicrobial properties. This can help keep your bento from spoiling before you have a chance to eat it.

Ginger Pork

FOR 2 BENTOS
PREPARATION TIME 10 MINUTES

1 tablespoon soy sauce
1 tablespoon sake
1/2 tablespoon sugar
1 teaspoon grated ginger
4 thin slices pork loin, total about 3 1/2 oz (100 g)
All-purpose flour, for dusting
2 teaspoons vegetable oil

1 Make the sauce by whisking together the soy sauce, sake, sugar and ginger in a small bowl.
2 Use a small sieve to dust both sides of each slice of pork with the flour.
3 Add the vegetable oil to a nonstick frying pan and lay the pork in the cold pan. Turn the heat to medium.
4 Fry the pork until golden brown on both sides.
5 Pour the sauce into the pan and boil, stirring, until the pork is coated with a shiny glaze.

How to pack the bento

Spread a portion of rice evenly across the bottom of the entire bento box and cover half of the rice with a leaf. Place the Ginger Pork on top of the leaf. Pack the Potato Salad into the top right corner of the bento box on top of the rice. Pack the Mini Bell Pepper Stir-fry over the remaining rice.

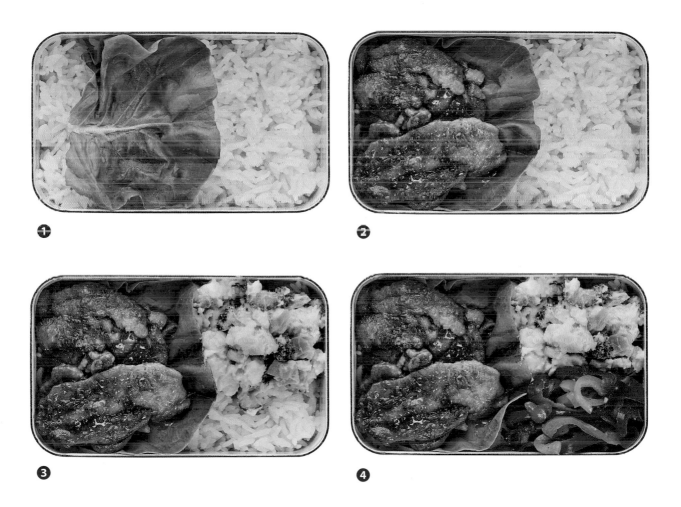

Miso Butter Chicken Bento | Marc

Shortly after coming to Japan, I moved up to Sapporo, on the northern island of Hokkaido. Though it snows for half of the year there, Hokkaido is the bread basket of Japan, producing the majority of the nation's domestic dairy products, potatoes and corn. It's also known for its miso ramen.

Inspired by the produce and flavors of the region, I started making Miso Butter — a compound butter mixed with miso paste to spread on grilled corn and smashed potatoes. It didn't take long to figure out that it was also amazing over pasta, with seafood or even slathered on crusty bread.

This stir-fry is one of my favorite ways to use Miso Butter because it pulls together the taste memories of my time in Hokkaido into a single easy dish. It also happens to be delicious in a bento!

Miso Butter
MAKES ABOUT 9 OZ (260 G)
PREPARATION TIME 5 MINUTES

This simple compound butter can be used as both a condiment and a seasoning. Whether you melt some over boiled corn, spread it in a sandwich or use it to season a stir fry, the rich butter and nutty miso are balanced out by the mild sweetness of the sugar. While mixing by hand works fine, if you want a smooth butter, use a food processor or hand blender.

1 stick (115 g) unsalted butter
¹/2 cup (145 g yellow miso paste
4 teaspoons sugar

1 Place the butter in a bowl and let it come to room temperature so that it softens.

2 Add the miso and sugar and whip together to blend. (Alternately, you can chop cold butter in a small food processor and then process it with the miso and sugar.)

3 Store unused Miso Butter in an airtight container in the refrigerator.

Miso Butter Chicken

FOR 2 BENTOS
PREPARATION TIME 10 MINUTES

1 small potato
1¹/2 skin-on chicken thighs, about 5¹/2 oz
  (150 g) total, cut into bite-sized pieces
Salt, to taste
Black pepper, to taste
2 teaspoons vegetable oil
4 stalks baby corn
1 small mild green chili pepper (Anaheim
  or Poblano), cored, seeded and chopped
2 tablespoons Miso Butter (see page 107)

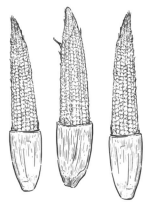

1 Bring a pot of water to a boil. Slice the potato into ¹/3-inch (8 mm) slices (use vegetable or cookie cutters to cut them into cute shapes if you like). Parboil the potatoes for 1 minute, then drain.

2 Sprinkle both sides of each piece of chicken with salt and pepper.

3 Preheat the pan over medium heat and swirl the oil around. Place the chicken skin-side down and fry until browned on one side.

4 Flip the chicken over. Arrange the potatoes and baby corn around the chicken.

5 When the chicken has browned on the second side, continue by stir-frying until the vegetables are cooked through.

6 Use a paper towel to wipe up any excess oil in the pan.

7 Add the peppers and Miso Butter and toss together until the Miso Butter has caramelized around everything.

How to pack the bento

Spread a portion of rice in a triangle shape in one corner of the bento box, and tuck a leaf into the corner to garnish. Fill the center of the box with a portion of Miso Butter Chicken. Place some leaves in front of the chicken to act as a partition and then fill the remaining space with fruit.

Sukiyaki Beef , Egg & Rice "Sandwich" | Maki

The rice balls called *onigiri* in Japanese (which roughly translates to "hand-formed") may be one of the most common bento items, but the triangular balls of rice require a bit of skill to make. *Onigirazu*, which means "NOT hand-formed" is a modern version of the onigiri that is made like a sandwich, with filling stuffed between two layers of rice and nori sheets. Because there is more room in the middle, the filling can be almost anything, making this a truly versatile bento item.

My youngest son helped me come up with the idea for this rice-sandwich recipe when he said, "I wish I could have some sukiyaki for my lunch." Sukiyaki, the Japanese hot pot, is usually made by cooking thinly sliced beef in a sweet and savory sauce, and it's served with raw egg for dipping. Hot pots aren't particularly well suited for bento, but by cooking the beef in our 3S Sauce and adding a fried egg, I was able to turn this classic hot pot into a rice sandwich that was a hit with both of my sons!

Bacon, Brussels Sprouts and Potatoes
FOR 2 BENTOS
PREPARATION TIME 10 MINUTES

¹/₂ tablespoon Infused Basil Oil (see page 39)
7 Brussels sprouts, trimmed and halved
1 small white potato, about 2 oz (50 g), peeled, diced and parboiled
1 slice bacon, cut into bite-sized pieces
1 teaspoon sake or white wine
Salt, to taste
Black pepper, to taste
1 teaspoon chopped parsley

1 Heat the Infused Basil Oil in a pan over medium heat.

2 Add the Brussels sprouts, potatoes and bacon and stir-fry.

3 When the Brussels sprouts start to brown, add the sake and cover with a lid.

4 When vegetables are tender, remove from heat. Season with salt and pepper to taste and garnish with the chopped parsley.

Sukiyaki Beef

FOR 2 RICE SANDWICHES
PREPARATION TIME 5 MINUTES

2 teaspoons vegetable oil
2 oz (50 g) thinly sliced beef
1 tablespoon 3S Sauce (see page 38)

1 Heat the oil in a pan over medium heat.
2 Fry the beef on both sides until it's just cooked through.
3 Add the 3S Sauce and boil until the sauce has caramelized around the meat.

Over-easy Eggs

FOR 2 RICE SANDWICHES
PREPARATION TIME 5 MINUTES

2 teaspoons vegetable oil
2 eggs
Salt, to taste
Black pepper, to taste

1 Heat the vegetable oil in a pan over medium-low heat.
2 Crack the eggs into opposite sides of the pan and fry until the whites are cooked through. Season with salt and pepper to taste.
3 Fold the eggs in half with a spatula and continue frying until the eggs are cooked through.

Sukiyaki Beef, Egg and Rice "Sandwich"

FOR 2 BENTOS
PREPARATION TIME 10 MINUTES

1¼ cups (250 g) cooked Basic White Rice (see page 36)
Salt, to taste
2 sheets nori
2 leaves lettuce
Sukiyaki Beef (see this page)
2 Over-easy Eggs (see this page)

1 Sprinkle the cooked rice with salt and gently mix.
2 Place each sheet of nori on a separate piece of plastic wrap.
3 Taking into account the size of the bento box, place a quarter of the rice in the center of each sheet of nori (picture 1).
4 Arrange a leaf of lettuce, half the Sukiyaki Beef and one Over-Easy Egg on each layer of rice (pictures 2, 3 and 4). Trim off the sides of the egg to fit on the rice if necessary.
5 Cover with the remaining rice and fold the corners of the nori over the rice (pictures 6 to 8). Wrap tightly with plastic wrap and allow to rest for ten minutes so the nori seals (picture 9).
6 Cut the rice sandwich in half with the plastic wrap on. Remove the wrap before packing the sandwich into the bento.

How to fold the Rice Sandwich

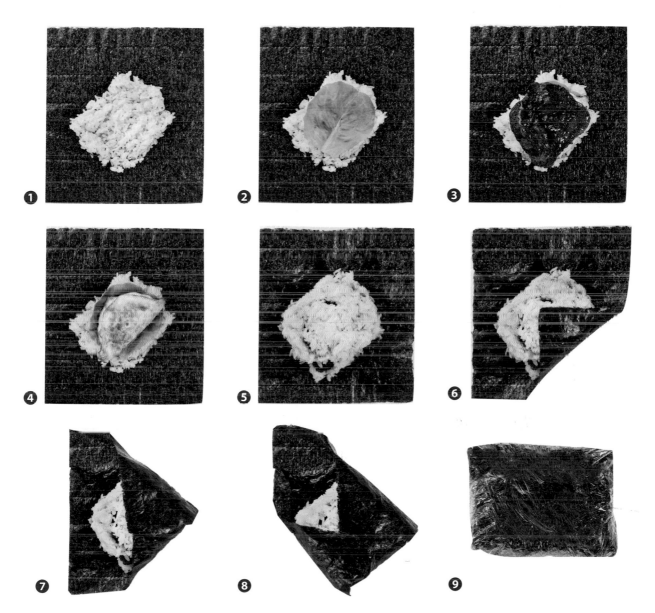

How to pack the bento

Place the two halves of the Sukiyaki Beef, Egg and Rice "Sandwich" in one half of the bento box. Place a leaf at the back of the empty space. Arrange a portion of Bacon, Brussels Sprouts and Potatoes in the top half of the empty space. Place another leaf as a partition in front of the Bacon, Brussels Sprouts and Potatoes and then fill the remaining space with fruit.

1

2

3

4

Ham and Cheese Roll Bento | Maki

In Japanese schools, there is a concept called *shokuiku*, which roughly translates as "food education." This isn't merely a nutrition class, but a core part of the curriculum that encourages the importance of eating well and enjoying food for a healthy, happy life. I'm a firm believer in this philosophy, and it's one of the reasons why I make bento for my sons.

In this spirit, I also encourage my kids to join me when I'm cooking, whenever I can. The Fun Ham and Cheese Rolls in this bento box are one of the dishes they love to make. These are a type of dim sum spring roll, but much simplified. It's a great recipe for kids; they can have lots of fun helping you stuff the rolls with their favorite ingredients. I hope you'll give these a try with your family!

Cucumber and Cauliflower with Infused Basil Oil

FOR 2 BENTOS
PREPARATION TIME 10 MINUTES

½ Japanese or Persian cucumber
4 small florets cauliflower, cut into bite-sized pieces
½ tablespoon Infused Basil Oil (see page 39)
Salt, to taste
Black pepper, to taste

1 Use a peeler to peel stripes into the cucumber.
2 Cut the cucumber into ½-inch (1 cm) thick rounds and sprinkle with salt. Set these aside for 10 minutes to sweat.
3 Boil the cauliflower for 2 minutes and drain.
4 Drain the moisture from the cucumber slices and toss them with the cauliflower and Infused Basil Oil. Season with salt and pepper to taste.

Fun Ham and Cheese Rolls

FOR 2 BENTOS
PREPARATION TIME 10 MINUTES

2 teaspoons all-purpose flour
2 teaspoons water
2 spring roll wrappers
2 thin slices ham
2 stalks asparagus, trimmed and boiled
2 slices American cheese
Vegetable oil, for deep-frying

1 Mix the flour and water to make a paste.

2 Place one wrapper on a flat surface with a corner pointing toward you (picture 1).

3 Place the cheese, ham and asparagus on the bottom half of the wrapper and roll them together (pictures 2 to 5).

4 Roll the bottom corner of the wrapper up and over the filling (picture 6).

5 Fold both sides of the wrapper toward the center (picture 7).

6 Continue rolling up. Spread a thin layer of flour-and-water paste across the top edges of the wrapper like you're going to seal an envelope (picture 8).

7 Finish rolling to seal the edges (picture 9). Repeat with the remaining wrapper and fillings. Save the leftover flour-and-water paste to make Cheese "Candies" (page 120).

8 Fry the rolls in vegetable oil that has been preheated to 340°F (170°C) until they are golden brown and crisp.

How to wrap the Ham and Cheese Rolls

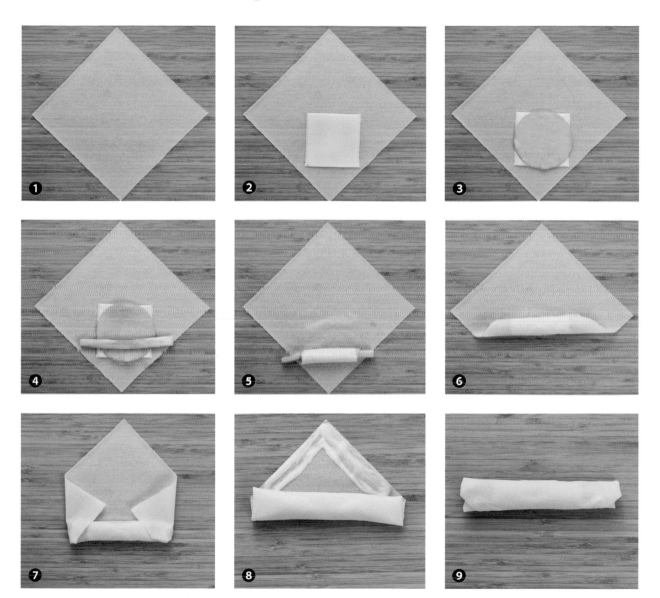

Cheese "Candies"

FOR 2 BENTOS
PREPARATION TIME 5 MINUTES

1 thin slice ham
4 cubes cheese, about ¹/2-inch (1 cm)
  square
1 spring roll wrapper
Leftover flour-and-water paste from
  Fun Ham and Cheese Rolls (page 118)

1 Use a straw to cut out circles from the sliced ham (picture 1). Place the dots of ham on the cheese.

2 Cut the wrapper into quarters (picture 2).

3 Place a cube of cheese in the center of each piece of wrapper (picture 3).

4 Spread a thin layer of flour-and-water paste on either side of each piece of cheese (picture 3).

5 Twist the wrapper around the cheese as though you are wrapping a piece of candy and press tightly to seal (pictures 4 and 5).

6 Fry the cheese candy as directed in the recipe for Fun Rolls until they are golden brown and crisp.

How to pack the bento

Spread a portion of rice evenly across the bottom two-thirds of the bento box and partition off the empty part of the box with leaves. Cut the Fun Ham and Cheese Rolls to fit and place them in the empty part of the box. Add the Cucumber and Cauliflower with Infused Basil Oil to fill the remaining space, and garnish with a cherry tomato. Place a leaf on the rice and top with a few Cheese "Candies."

Pan-fried Wasabi Chicken Bento | Maki

If you thought wasabi only goes well with sushi, think again! In Japan, wasabi is a potent seasoning used to add a kick to salad dressings, noodles and even meat. For this bento, I've used the classic combination of soy sauce and wasabi to season pan-fried chicken. Cooking the wasabi allows the compounds responsible for the spicy taste to burn off, making this dish suitable for kids' bento boxes as well. If you want to retain some of the spiciness, just add a little extra wasabi at the end, after you've removed the chicken from the heat.

Pan-fried Wasabi Chicken

FOR 3 BENTOS
PREPARATION TIME 15 MINUTES

**2 skin-on chicken thighs, about 7 oz
   (200 g) total, trimmed and cut into bite-
   sized pieces**
Salt, to taste
Black pepper, to taste
1 tablespoon all-purpose flour
2 teaspoons butter
1¹/2 tablespoons soy sauce
1 tablespoon sake or white wine
¹/2 tablespoon wasabi paste

1 Season the chicken with salt and pepper, then dust it with an even sprinkling of flour.
2 Melt the butter in a pan and fry the chicken until golden brown on both sides.
3 Whisk together the soy sauce, sake and wasabi and pour over the chicken. Boil until the sauce thickens into a shiny glaze.

Wasabi

Wasabi is a condiment made by grating the rhizome of an aquatic plant by the same name. It's in the same family as mustard and horseradish, and the pungent spicy taste of wasabi is caused by the same volatile compound present in its relatives: allyl isothiocyanate.

In the same way that mustard and horseradish have a different flavor, wasabi has a unique aroma that sets it apart from its relatives. Unfortunately, true wasabi is notoriously difficult to grow which makes it very expensive.

This is why most products sold as "wasabi" outside of Japan are actually made with mustard or horseradish combined with color and flavor additives.

Kinpira Carrots

FOR 3 BENTOS

PREPARATION TIME 5 MINUTES

1 teaspoon vegetable oil
2-inch (5 cm) length carrot, about 2 oz
  (50 g), cut into matchsticks
1 tablespoon 3S Sauce (see page 38)
Toasted white sesame seeds, for garnish

1 Heat oil in a nonstick frying pan. Add carrots and sauté until tender.

2 Add the 3S Sauce and boil until the liquid has evaporated.

3 Garnish with the sesame seeds.

How to pack the bento

Fill one-third of the bento box with rice and then taper the rice down the center third of the box, adding a leaf to garnish. Arrange some Pan-fried Wasabi Chicken on top of the leaf. Add some Kinpira Carrots next to the chicken. Use more leaves to create a partition in the front corner of the bento box and tuck some fruit into the space created.

Hanami Bento | Marc

Starting in the south and moving north as the temperature warms, a flurry of pastel cherry blossoms explode in Japan every year between March and May. This magical season is fleeting, but people make the most of it by celebrating the blooming of cherry blossoms through *hanami*, or flower viewing. Like most traditional activities in Japan, hanami has a long and complicated history, but these days, it's a great excuse to have a picnic and a few drinks under flowering cherry trees with friends and family.

A hanami bento is usually packed with spring delicacies, but I've taken a more literal approach with this bento by putting the flowers into the box! You can enjoy this bowl of spring any time of the year. Or, you can use it as a template to build your own seasonal scene using shapes, colors and ingredients that reflect the season.

Pickled Root-vegetable Flowers

FOR 2 BENTOS
PREPARATION TIME 2 MINUTES
MARINATION TIME 30 MINUTES TO 24 HOURS

2 rounds daikon, cut ¹/₄-inch (5 mm) thick
8 rounds carrot, cut ¹/₄-inch (5 mm) thick
1 tablespoon Sushi Vinegar (see page 38)

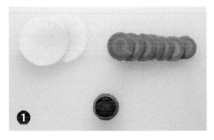

1 Use cookie or vegetable cutters to cut the daikon and carrot slices into flower shapes (pictures 1 and 2).
2 Place the flower slices in a small bowl and cover with Sushi Vinegar. Allow to marinate for at least 30 minutes. Can be prepared up to a day in advance.

Sesame Sushi Rice

FOR 2 BENTOS
PREPARATION TIME 30 MINUTES

2 tablespoons toasted sesame seeds
2 servings Sushi Rice (see page 37)

1 Prepare the Sushi Rice following the recipe on page 37 (pictures 1 and 2).
2 Grind the sesame seeds with a mortar and pestle. Alternately, you can use a clean spice grinder, blender or food processor.
3 Add the ground sesame seeds to the sushi rice and fold to distribute evenly (pictures 3 and 4).

Lemon Broccoli and Asparagus

FOR 2 BENTOS
PREPARATION TIME 4 MINUTES

2 large florets broccoli, about 2¹/₂ oz (75 g),
  cut into bite-sized pieces
6 thin spears asparagus, trimmed
1 teaspoon olive oil
Zest of ¹/₂ lemon
Salt, to taste

1 Bring a pot of salted water to a boil and blanch the broccoli and asparagus for 1 to 2 minutes.
2 Drain the vegetables well, shaking off any excess water.
3 Toss the broccoli and asparagus with the olive oil and lemon zest. Season with salt to taste.

Hanami Bento

FOR 2 BENTOS
PREPARATION TIME 2 MINUTES

2 servings Sesame Sushi Rice (see facing page)
2 slices ham
2 slices American cheese
2 servings Lemon Broccoli and Asparagus (see facing page)
2 servings Pickled Root-vegetable Flowers (see page 127)

1 Divide the rice between two bento boxes. Spread rice along the bottom of each bento box, leaving a groove in the side closest to you (picture 1).

2 Use cookie or vegetable cutters to cut the ham and cheese into flower shapes. Scatter them around the upper three-quarters of the rice (picture 2).

3 Arrange the Lemon Broccoli and Asparagus in the groove along the bottom (picture 3). Top each bento with Pickled Root-Vegetable flowers (picture 4).

①

②

③

④

Kushiage Chicken Skewer Bento | Marc

Inspiration comes in many forms — I got the idea for this bento on a bar crawl in Kobe! Our first stop was a diminutive standing bar with wooden counters facing the sidewalk. There was just enough room inside for the older gentleman frying skewers to make his magic happen. Although they all looked alike, each crispy skewer that landed on my plate contained a different surprise beneath the breading. It was fun and effortless to pop each morsel into my mouth from the skewer. "Perfect for bento!" I thought.

Kushiage, which literally means "fried skewer," is not a common bento item, but if you think about the qualities that make food work in a bento — things like being delicious and satisfying, having a low moisture content and being easy to eat — kushiage is a natural fit.

Since the breading covers the food, I've left a few of the vegetables in the bento naked to add a little more color. I've also used mustard-green rice — an easy way to make rice more interesting while incorporating additional veggies.

Shiozuke Salt Pickles

Like many countries with harsh winters, Japan developed a culture of pickling and preserving vegetables. Today the pickled-foods section of a Japanese grocery store is a rainbow of produce, from cucumbers and cabbage to turnips and tomatoes.

Shiozuke (salt pickles), made by salting vegetables, are the most basic type of pickle. They're called *asazuke* (lightly pickled) when they're relatively fresh; once they have undergone lacto-fermentation they are known as *furuzuke* (old pickles).

The Pickled Mustard Greens recipe (overleaf) is used in the rice for this bento, but the same brine works with almost any vegetable to make salt pickles to pack as a side.

Pickled Mustard Greens

FOR 2 BENTOS
PICKLING TIME 1 DAY

1 tablespoon salt
2 cups (480 ml) water
1 dried chili pepper, optional
1 small piece kombu seaweed, optional
Small bunch mustard greens, about 3 oz (85 g)

1 Dissolve the salt in the water. Add the chili pepper and kombu (picture 1), and the mustard greens (picture 2). Completely cover the greens in the water. Let stand for at least 24 hours.
2 When ready to use the greens, drain, and squeeze out the excess water with your hands.

Mustard-green Rice

FOR 2 BENTOS
PREPARATION TIME 30 MINUTES

2 servings Basic White Rice (see page 36)
2 servings Pickled Mustard Greens

1 Follow the directions to make the rice.
2 Wring out as much liquid as you can from the greens and mince them finely (pictures 1 and 2).
3 When the rice is done steaming, fold the minced pickles into the hot rice (picture 3).

Panko Breading

Many deep-fried items — from *ebi-furai* (fried shrimp) to *tonkatsu* (pork cutlets) to *korokke* (croquettes) — are breaded in panko breadcrumbs using this quick and easy method.

1 In three separate bowls, have ready all-purpose flour, a beaten egg and panko breadcrumbs (picture 1).

2 Dust the food to be breaded with a thin, even coating of flour (picture 2).

3 Dip the food in the egg, ensuring that there are no dry spots (picture 3).

4 Roll the food in the panko, pressing gently to make sure the breadcrumbs adhere well to the surface (picture 4).

Kushiage Skewers

FOR 2 BENTOS
PREPARATION TIME 20 MINUTES

1¹/₂ skin-on chicken thighs, about 5¹/₂ oz
  (150 g) total, trimmed and cut into 1-inch
  (2.5 cm) pieces
¹/₂ onion, about 3 oz (85 g), peeled,
  trimmed and cut into 1-inch (2.5 cm) cubes
2 slices lotus root, cut ¹/₃-inch (8 mm) thick
2 slices kabocha or butternut squash, cut
  ¹/₃ inch (8 mm) thick
4 ears baby corn
4 stalks asparagus
Salt
Black pepper
¹/₄ cup (30 g) all-purpose flour
1 large egg, beaten
³/₄ cup (45 g) panko breadcrumbs
Vegetable oil, for deep frying
Tonkatsu Sauce (see page 39)

1 Use toothpicks to skewer one piece of chicken with a similar-sized piece of onion. Skewer the lotus root and squash separately (picture 1). The baby corn and asparagus should not be breaded or skewered.

2 Season the skewered items with salt and pepper (picture 2).

3 In a heavy-bottomed pot or deep pan, preheat 2 inches (5 cm) of vegetable oil to 340°F (170°C).

4 Bread the skewers (picture 3) as directed on page 133.

5 Fry the asparagus in the oil for just a few seconds, until it's a vibrant green. Fry the baby corn until it's golden brown.

6 Fry the skewers until golden brown. Drain on a rack lined with paper towels (picture 4).

7 Let the skewers cool completely before packing them into the bento. Finish them off with a drizzle of Tonkatsu Sauce.

How to make the Kushiage Skewers

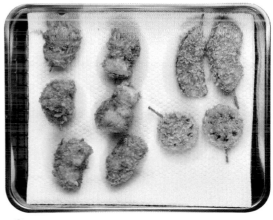

Tempura Donburi Bento | Maki

Tempura might seem like one of those dishes you're more likely to order at a restaurant than make at home, but it's surprisingly easy to put together yourself. On weekends, I often make tempura from odds and ends in the fridge. Root vegetables such as carrots and potatoes work great, and dense veggies such as kabocha or butternut squash work well too. Although I prefer making vegetable tempura, you'll find that seafood and meat (like chicken tenders) work well too.

There are a few keys to making light, crisp tempura. First, use ice water in the batter. Also, be careful not to overmix it; small lumps are fine. Dusting the ingredients with flour helps the batter adhere to the food as it cooks. Finally, fry your battered items in oil at about 340°F (170°C); this keeps the batter from browning too quickly

For this bento, I serve the tempura over a bed of rice to make a tempura *donburi* (rice bowl), or *ten-don* for short. The sweet and savory Ten-don Sauce trickles down into the rice, making it irresistible all the way to the last bite!

Lemon-pickled Radishes

FOR 2 BENTOS
PREPARATION TIME 5 MINUTES
PICKLING TIME 8 HOURS

5 to 6 globe radishes
1 teaspoon lemon juice
1/4 teaspoon salt

1 Cut the radishes in half and place them in a zipper bag. Add the lemon juice and salt and massage lightly.
2 Allow the radishes to pickle in the refrigerator for 8 hours or overnight.

Ten-don Sauce

FOR 2 BENTOS
PREPARATION TIME 2 MINUTES

1 tablespoon soy sauce
2 tablespoons sake
2 tablespoons sugar

1 Combine all ingredients in a saucepan and bring to a boil over high heat.
2 Turn the heat down and simmer until the sauce has thickened slightly (about 20 seconds).

Seafood and Vegetable Tempura

FOR 2 BENTOS
PREPARATION TIME 25 MINUTES

2 slices kabocha or butternut squash, cut ⅓-inch (8 mm) thick
2 slices potato, cut ⅓-inch (8 mm) thick
2 stalks asparagus, top half only
2 imitation crab sticks
4 small pieces white-fleshed fish, such as cod, about ½ oz (15 g) each
6 tablespoons cake flour, plus more for dusting
5 tablespoons ice water
Vegetable oil, for deep-frying

1 Dust all ingredients with flour (picture 1).

2 Combine the 6 tablespoons of flour and the ice water in a bowl and mix briefly (picture 2). The batter should resemble thin pancake batter (a few lumps are fine); adjust by adding more water or flour as needed (picture 3).

3 Heat the oil to 340°F (170°C).

4 Dip each ingredient in batter, then transfer to the oil and fry until cooked through (pictures 4, 5 and 6). Drain on a paper towel-lined rack.

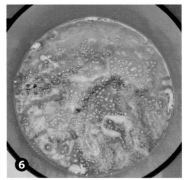

How to pack the bento

Spread a portion of rice evenly across the bottom of the bento box, leaving one corner empty. Place a leaf in the empty corner to create a partition. Place the Seafood and Vegetable Tempura pieces on top of the rice, layering them from back to front. Place some Lemon Pickled Radishes in the empty corner. Drizzle the Ten-don Sauce all over the tempura.

Grilled Salmon and Omelet Bento | Maki

The rolled omelet known as *tamagoyaki* is a home-cooked favorite in Japan. It's eaten for breakfast, lunch or even dinner, and it makes for a protein-packed splash of color in a bento box. While sweet tamagoyaki and *dashimaki tamago* (rolled omelet seasoned with dashi stock) are popular variations on this classic, I'm going to introduce you to one of my younger son's favorites, Rainbow Omelet, which I make with odds and ends from the refrigerator. This recipe uses cheese, sausage and green beans, but you can make it with green onions, spinach, bacon or anything you happen to have on hand.

Tamagoyaki is traditionally cooked in layers that are rolled in a shallow rectangular tamagoyaki pan (see page 20), which makes the omelet attractive and uniform in shape. Since it's not always easy to find these pans outside of Japan, this recipe shows how to make the omelet with a round frying pan and some plastic wrap.

Grilled Salmon

FOR 2 BENTOS
PREPARATION TIME 7 TO 8 MINUTES
MARINATING TIME 8 HOURS

1 teaspoon salt
2 salmon fillets, each about 3¹/2 oz (100 g)
 and ¹/2-inch (1 cm) thick

1 Sprinkle the salt evenly over both sides of the salmon.
2 Line a tray with a clean lint-free towel and place the salmon on it.

3 Place another towel on top of the salmon. Cover the tray with plastic wrap and refrigerate overnight.
4 Broil the cured salmon in the oven or pan-fry it in a little oil.

Rainbow Omelet

FOR 2 BENTOS
PREPARATION TIME 10 MINUTES

2 eggs
2 tablespoons leftover green vegetables,
  sausage and/or cheese, finely diced
Salt, to taste
Black pepper, to taste
Vegetable oil, for frying

1 Combine the eggs and diced filling
ingredients in a bowl and season with salt
and pepper (picture 1). Beat gently until
the egg is uniform in color.

2 Dampen a paper towel with oil and use
it to oil a nonstick pan while preheating
over medium-low heat (picture 2).

3 When the pan is hot, add a third of the
egg mixture. Swirl it around the pan to
spread evenly (picture 3).

4 Once it's almost cooked through, use a
spatula to roll the egg to one side of the
pan (pictures 4 and 5).

5 Repeat steps 3 and 4, adding each layer
to the roll of egg, until all the egg is gone.

6 Wrap the cooked omelet tightly in
plastic wrap and shape into a rectangular
block while it's hot (pictures 6 and 7).

7 When it has cooled, unwrap the omelet
and cut it into 1-inch (2.5 cm) slices.

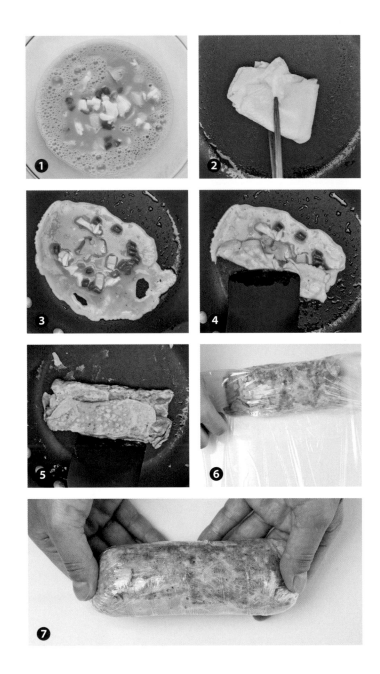

How to pack the bento

Spread a portion of rice evenly across the bottom of the entire bento box and top a section of the rice with leaves. Place a piece of Grilled Salmon on the rice. Add three pieces of Rainbow Omelet on top of the leaves. Fill the spaces with cherry tomatoes.

1

2

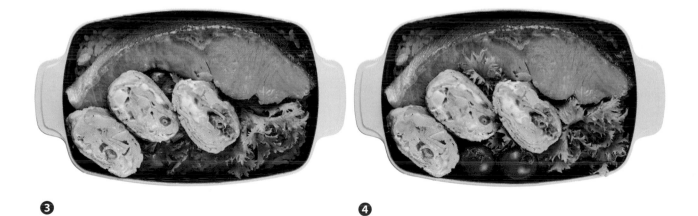

3

4

Chili Shrimp Bento | Marc

Just as the US has Chinese-American inventions like chop suey and General Tso's chicken, Japan has *ebi chiri* (chili shrimp). It was created in the 1950s by a Chinese chef living in Japan named Chen Kenmin. Chef Chen wanted to introduce a taste of his home province of Sichuan to his Japanese customers, but most Japanese at that time were not used to spicy foods. To appeal to the local populace, the chef added ketchup to sweeten the sauce and impart a vibrant hue that makes it look far spicier than it actually is.

The thought of altering a dish with ketchup to satisfy local customers sounds like a travesty, and I have to say I was a bit skeptical the first time I tried this dish. But if you stop to think about it, this is how food evolves around the world. In Japan, it's led to a whole genre of Japanese-style Chinese food including dishes like ramen, *gyoza* dumplings and *karaage* fried chicken. Can you imagine a world without ramen because someone sneered at the idea of adapting Chinese noodles to suit local tastes?

As it turns out, the spicy, sweet and tangy flavor combo is heavenly, and chili shrimp has become one of my favorite dishes to order at Chinese restaurants in Japan. I've turned it into a simple stir-fry for this bento and paired it with crisp Pickled Lotus Root, Roast Shishito Peppers and a comfortingly simple Egg Fried Rice.

Egg Fried Rice
FOR 2 BENTOS
PREPARATION TIME 5 MINUTES

1 tablespoon vegetable oil
2 servings cooked Basic White Rice (see page 36)
1 teaspoon soy sauce
1/2 teaspoon onion powder
Salt, to taste
White pepper, to taste
1 egg, beaten

1 Heat a nonstick frying pan over medium-high heat and add the oil.
2 When the oil is hot, add the rice and stir-fry, breaking up any clumps as you go.
3 When the rice is hot, add the soy sauce and onion powder. Season with salt and pepper to taste and stir until the mixture is uniform in color.
4 Pour the egg over the rice and quickly stir the mixture to keep it from clumping up. The fried rice is done when the egg is cooked to your liking.

Chili Shrimp

FOR 2 BENTOS
PREPARATION TIME 15 MINUTES

7 oz (200 g) peeled deveined
  shrimp
¹/₂ small egg white
2 teaspoons potato starch, divided
2 tablespoons water
2 tablespoons ketchup
1 teaspoon doubanjiang chili paste
¹/₂ teaspoon toasted sesame oil
1 tablespoon vegetable oil
2 tablespoons minced green onions
  (scallions), white part only
1 teaspoon minced ginger
1 small clove garlic, minced
1 teaspoon rice vinegar

1 Combine the shrimp, egg white and 1¹/₂
teaspoons of the potato starch in a bowl
(picture 1). Mix together vigorously by hand
(picture 2) until the egg white is slightly
foamy (picture 3). Set aside to marinate
while you prepare the other ingredients.

2 To make the sauce, whisk together the
water, ketchup, doubanjiang, remaining ¹/₂
teaspoon of potato starch, and sesame oil in
a small bowl.

3 Remove the shrimp from the marinade
and pat dry with a paper towel.

4 Heat a frying pan over medium-high heat.
Add the vegetable oil and swirl to coat the pan.

5 Add the shrimp in a single layer. When they
are halfway cooked, flip them over.

6 Add the green onion, ginger and garlic to the
pan and stir-fry until the aromatics are fragrant.

7 Pour the sauce mixture into the pan and toss
to coat the shrimp evenly. When the sauce is
thick and glossy, remove the pan from the heat
and stir in the rice vinegar.

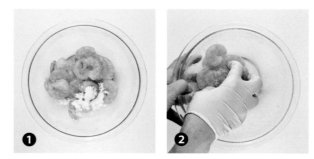

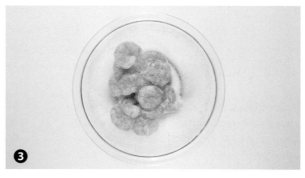

Roast Shishito Peppers

FOR 2 BENTOS
PREPARATION TIME 3 MINUTES

10 shishito peppers or other mild
green chilis
1 teaspoon oil
Sea salt, to taste

1 Wash and dry the peppers thoroughly. Poke holes in the chilis with the tip of a knife.
2 Heat the oil in a small nonstick frying pan over high heat.
3 Add the peppers and fry without stirring until they are browned on one side, about 1 minute.
4 Turn the peppers over and brown the other side. Sprinkle with sea salt and transfer to a plate to cool.

Pickled Lotus Root

FOR 2 BENTOS
PICKLING TIME 8 HOURS

4 slices lotus root, about 2 oz (50 g) total,
prepared as directed in the next column
3 tablespoons Sushi Vinegar (see
page 38)

1 Bring a pot of salted water to a boil. Add the lotus root and boil for 2 minutes.
2 Drain the lotus root. Place in a container, cover with the Sushi Vinegar and marinate overnight.

Velveting

Velveting is a Chinese method of marinating proteins with egg white and potato starch. This technique is used in the Chili Shrimp recipe on the facing page, and it's worth noting because it can be applied to many dishes to improve the texture of proteins while preventing them from drying out. For shrimp, velveting imparts a snap that's a bit like biting through the casing of a great sausage, while leaving the meat plump and juicy.

How to Prepare Lotus Root

The lotus is one of those precious plants whose every part has a use. The fragrant leaves impart their flavor to rice when steamed with it. The seeds can be eaten raw or cooked; the stems are delicious in stir-fries; the flowers can be made into tea. Perhaps the most renowned part of the lotus is the tubular "root" (actually a rhizome), which has a beautiful pattern of holes that can be stuffed, or sliced and cut to resemble a flower or a snowflake. Lotus roots are like sunchokes in texture and taste, and are best cooked lightly to preserve their crisp texture.

1 Peel the lotus root with a vegetable peeler.
2 Slice crosswise into rounds, exposing the pattern of holes.
3 Cut lotus root oxidizes quickly. Soak the slices in water with a little lemon juice or vinegar to prevent discoloring.
4 Carve around the holes to make flower shapes or cut V-shaped pieces out of the perimeter to make snowflakes.

Chicken and Egg Soboro Bento | Maki

Called *sanshoku soboro* in Japanese (*sanshoku* means "three colors" and *soboro* means "crumbled") this is a classic bento that's easy to make and delicious! Soboro usually refers to bits of seasoned meat, fish or egg layered on top of rice. The various colors and small crumbles make it easy to create patterns in a bento. I like adding different vegetables to vary the colors while making the bento more nutritionally balanced.

To assemble this bento, I use clean rubber bands to divide the box into six sections. This makes it easy to create a mosaic pattern with clean straight lines and alternating colors. I've used a combination of chicken soboro, egg soboro and a snap pea stir-fry in this bento box, but you can get creative by using ingredients like flaked salmon, asparagus and purple cabbage to create grids of contrasting colors.

Snap Pea Stir-fry
FOR 2 BENTOS
PREPARATION TIME 3 MINUTES

1 teaspoon vegetable oil
8 to 10 snap peas, trimmed and halved
Dash garlic powder
Salt, to taste
Black pepper, to taste

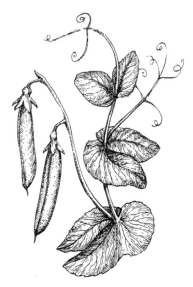

1 Heat the oil in a pan over medium heat.
2 Stir-fry the snap peas until they're cooked through.
3 Season with garlic powder, salt and pepper to taste.

Chicken Soboro

FOR 2 BENTOS
PREPARATION TIME 3 MINUTES

2 tablespoons 3S Sauce (see page 38)
3 oz (85 g) ground chicken

1 Pour the 3S Sauce into a pan and bring it to a boil.
2 Add the ground chicken, breaking it apart with chopsticks or a spatula (picture 1).
3 Lower the heat and simmer until there is no liquid left in the pan (picture 2).

Egg Soboro

FOR 2 BENTOS
PREPARATION TIME 3 MINUTES

2 teaspoons butter
2 eggs, beaten
Salt, to taste
White pepper, to taste

1 Melt the butter in a nonstick pan over medium-low heat.
2 Pour the beaten egg into the pan (picture 1) and scramble it with a spatula (picture 2).
3 Season with salt and pepper to taste.
4 Crumble the egg with a fork to make the soboro (picture 3).

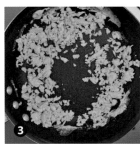

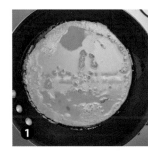

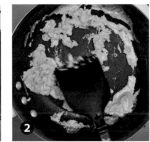

How to pack the bento

Spread a portion of rice evenly across the bottom of the box. Use three clean rubber bands to partition the box into six sections. Place Chicken Soboro in two alternating segments. Place Egg Soboro in another two alternating segments. Place Snap Pea Stir-fry in the remaining two segments. If you like you can garnish the bento with sesame seeds and Sausage Octopuses (see page 49).

❶

❷

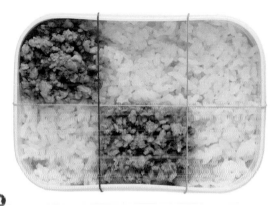

❸

❹

Maitake Mushroom Steak Bento | Marc

While most plant-based meat alternatives can tick either the texture box or the flavor box, it's rare to find an ingredient that can accomplish both. *Maitake*, or hen-of-the-woods mushroom (*Grifola frondosa*), is a polypore mushroom with a texture that closely mimics the muscle fibers found in meat. It also has an intensely savory and meaty flavor, which makes it a brilliant meat substitute for vegetarians and vegans.

Maitake also has another hidden superpower: it's one of the few food-based sources of vitamin D, a vital nutrient that's essential for calcium absorption and bone growth.

I like to pan-sear clusters of maitake using a weight on top to press them flat as they cook. This not only ensures a nice crust, but it also flattens out the frilly caps, making the clusters look like steaks. A splash of 3S Sauce gives the steak a savory-sweet teriyaki glaze that makes this one of the most flavorful bento meals in this book. Served over a bed of edamame rice, with Quick Pickled Red Cabbage and Sesame Green Beans, this is a mouthwatering protein-packed bento that even non-vegans can get behind.

Sesame Green Beans
FOR 2 BENTOS
PREPARATION TIME 10 MINUTES

10 green beans
1 tablespoon toasted sesame seeds
1/2 teaspoon soy sauce
1/4 teaspoon sugar

1 Trim and cut the green beans into 1-inch (2.5 cm) pieces.

2 Blanch the green beans in well-salted boiling water until they are bright green and tender, but not mushy. Drain and immediately shock in ice water to set their color.
3 Grind the sesame seeds with a mortar and pestle, clean spice grinder, blender or food processor.
4 Mix green beans, ground sesame seeds, soy sauce and sugar. Toss to coat evenly.

Maitake Mushroom Steaks

FOR 2 BENTOS
PREPARATION TIME 10 MINUTES

**2 large clusters maitake mushrooms,
  about 3 oz (85 g) each**
2 tablespoons vegetable oil
3 tablespoons 3S Sauce (see page 38)

1 Drizzle each piece of maitake with 1 tablespoon of vegetable oil on all sides.

2 Heat a skillet over medium heat. Put the mushrooms in the pan (picture 1) and set a heavy pan (such as a cast-iron skillet) on top of the mushrooms to flatten them (picture 2).

3 Fry the mushrooms undisturbed until they are golden brown and crisp on one side (about 5 minutes).

4 Remove the weight and flip each mushroom steak over. Place the weight on top of them again and continue to fry until golden brown and crisp on the second side (picture 3).

5 Remove the weight and add the 3S Sauce. Raise the heat to high and boil the sauce into a thick, shiny glaze, turning the maitake over repeatedly to coat it evenly. Continue cooking until almost no sauce is left, being careful not to burn the glaze (picture 4).

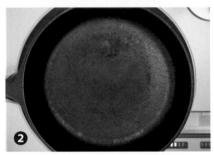

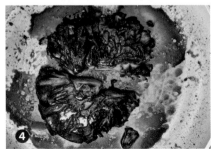

Quick Pickled Red Cabbage

FOR 2 BENTOS
PREPARATION TIME 20 MINUTES

1 leaf red cabbage, about 2 oz (50 g)
1 tablespoon Sushi Vinegar (see page 38)
Pinch of salt

1 Remove the thick stem from the cabbage and cut the leaf into quarters.
2 Stack and roll the pieces and use a sharp knife to slice the cabbage into thin threads.
3 Put the cabbage in a bowl along with the Sushi Vinegar and salt and massage the mixture together. Allow to marinate for at least 15 minutes.
4 Lightly squeeze any excess liquid out of the cabbage before packing it into the bento.

Quick Pickles

Pickles are usually made by salting vegetables and letting them ferment over several days or even weeks. The salt draws out water from the vegetables, and then salt-tolerant microbes like *Lactobacillus* convert naturally occurring sugars into lactic acid, giving the veggies a sour taste.

Since most of us don't want to wait too long, quick pickling is a great way to make an easy tangy side dish for your bento box in less than twenty minutes. The best part is that the vinegar helps preserve the vegetables, so the pickles can be made ahead of time and stored in the fridge for use throughout the week.

While this works well for many vegetables, including cucumbers, carrots and celery; I especially like making quick pickles with vegetables like beets, red cabbage and red onions because the low pH of the vinegar turns the pigments in the produce a vibrant shade of red.

Edamame Rice

FOR 2 BENTOS
PREPARATION TIME 35 MINUTES

³/4 cup (150 g) uncooked Japanese short-grain white rice
1 cup (240 ml) water
¹/4 teaspoon salt
¹/3 cup (125 g) cooked shelled edamame beans
¹/2 pouch, about ¹/2 oz (15 g), abura-age deep-fried tofu, diced

1 Put the rice in a strainer and rinse under cold water. Use your hand to agitate the rice until the water runs clear.

2 Place the drained rice in a deep pot along with the water, salt and abura-age. Stir to combine and then cover with a lid. For the best texture, let stand for 30 minutes before cooking.

3 When you're ready to cook the rice, set the pot over high heat and bring to a boil. Reduce the heat to low and set a timer for 12 minutes.

4 When the timer goes off, turn off the heat and let the rice steam for another 15 minutes without opening the lid. When the rice is done steaming, fold the shelled edamame into the rice.

How to pack the bento

Spread a portion of Edamame Rice evenly across two-thirds of the bento box. Top the rice with a Maitake Mushroom Steak. Use a leaf to partition the rice from the empty space and then fill half of the space with a portion of Sesame Green Beans. Add another leaf to partition the Sesame Green Beans from the remaining space, and fill that space with some Quick Pickled Red Cabbage.

❶

❷

❸

❹

Omurice Bento | Marc

Modern Japanese cuisine is a patchwork of foods from around the world reinterpreted in a way that's uniquely Japanese. This dish, called *omuraisu* in Japan — a portmanteau of "omelet" and "rice"— is an excellent example of *yoshoku* or Western-style Japanese cuisine. It may look like an omelet on the outside, but inside it's filled with savory-sweet fried rice.

The mild flavors and simple preparation have made "omurice" (as I call it here) a comfort-food staple in Japan; and the smooth surface of the egg is a perfect blank canvas to draw shapes such as a heart, a star or even a face, using ketchup.

Some versions of omurice top the fried rice with a creamy layer of partially cooked eggs, but this is not safe for a bento. I've used an egg crepe to wrap the fried rice. This type of thin omelet is a useful way to add both protein and color to a bento. Not only can it be used as a sheet to wrap food, but you can cut shapes in it with cookie cutters or slice it into thin golden threads to create a stunning garnish.

Carrot and Tuna Salad
FOR 2 BENTOS
PREPARATION TIME 12 MINUTES

2¹/₂-inch (6 cm) length carrot, about 2¹/₂ oz (75 g), grated or cut into thin matchsticks
¹/₈ teaspoon salt, plus more for seasoning
2 tablespoons canned tuna in oil
1 teaspoon olive oil
1 teaspoon chopped parsley
Pepper, to taste

1 Sprinkle the carrot with the salt and toss to distribute evenly. Set aside for 10 minutes while you combine the remaining ingredients in a bowl.

3 Massage the carrots to coax out any excess water and then use your hands to squeeze out as much water as you can.

4 Add the carrots to the bowl and toss. Season with additional salt and pepper.

Tomato-marinated Eggplant

FOR 2 BENTOS
PREPARATION TIME 12 MINUTES

2 tablespoons olive oil
¹/4 onion, about 1 oz (30 g), cut into 1-inch
  (2.5 cm) dice
1 small Japanese eggplant, cut into
  ¹/2-inch (1 cm) dice
8 cherry tomatoes
2 tablespoons chopped celery
¹/2 tablespoon capers
1¹/2 tablespoons Sushi Vinegar (see page 38)
Black pepper, to taste

1 Heat the oil in a small nonstick frying pan over medium heat. Add the onions and eggplant. Fry until the eggplant is golden brown.
2 Poke each tomato with a knife and add to the pan. Stir-fry until they have dissolved.
3 Add the celery, capers, Sushi Vinegar and black pepper. Continue stir-frying until the eggplant is coated in a thick sauce.

Egg Crepe

MAKES 2 SHEETS
PREPARATION TIME 10 MINUTES

Called *usuyaki tamago* in Japanese, this is a thin sheet of egg that can be used to wrap fillings or cut to create colorful garnishes. To make an omelet with a beautiful gold hue, you'll need to start with an egg that has a vibrant orange yolk. Then it must be cooked over a low heat so that it doesn't brown. A nonstick frying pan is essential, as eggs tend to stick to a cool pan.

1 egg
Pinch of salt

1 Break the egg into a bowl. Use chopsticks or tweezers to remove the ropy white parts near the yolk (picture 1).
2 Add the salt and beat the egg until it is uniform in color. Try to avoid incorporating air, as this will create unwanted bubbles (pictures 2 and 3).
3 Use a paper towel to lightly oil a nonstick frying pan (picture 4). Place the pan over medium-low heat until it is moderately hot.
4 Add half of the egg and swirl it around to coat the bottom of the pan evenly. Reduce heat to low and allow to cook slowly until the egg is almost completely cooked through (picture 5).
5 Flip the egg over and cook for a few seconds more until it is fully set (picture 6). Repeat steps 4 and 5 with the remaining beaten egg.

How to make the Egg Crepe

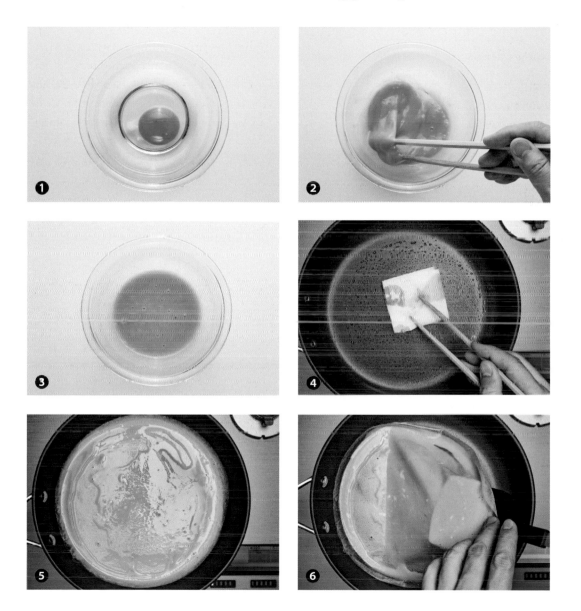

Omurice

MAKES 2 BENTOS
PREPARATION TIME 25 MINUTES

¹/2 chicken breast, about 4 oz (120 g), cut into
  ¹/2-inch (1 cm) dice
1 teaspoon soy sauce
1 tablespoon vegetable oil
¹/4 small onion, finely minced
2 servings cooked Basic White Rice (page 36)
2 tablespoons ketchup
1 tablespoon oyster sauce
Black pepper, to taste
2 sheets Egg Crepe (see page 160)

1 Marinate the chicken in the soy sauce while
heating the oil in a frying pan on medium heat. Add
the onion. Sauté till tender and turning brown. Add
the chicken. Stir-fry till there are no raw edges.

2 Add the rice and continue to cook, breaking
up any clumps as you go. When the rice is hot,
add the ketchup, oyster sauce and black pepper.
Stir together until the rice is an even color.

3 While the rice is hot, place two large sheets of
plastic wrap on a work surface. Lay one sheet of
Egg Crepe on each sheet of wrap.

4 Split the rice between the centers of both
Egg Crepes (picture 1). Fold the egg over the
rice, starting from the top and working your way
around counter-clockwise (pictures 2 to 5).

5 Wrap the omelets tightly in plastic wrap. Let
cool completely before unwrapping (picture 6).

6 Once in the bento box, you can slice an X into
the top and fold the flaps out to reveal the rice
underneath.

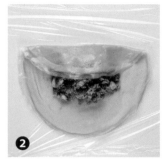
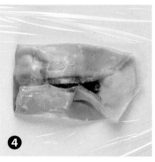
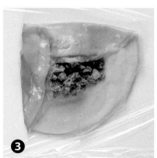
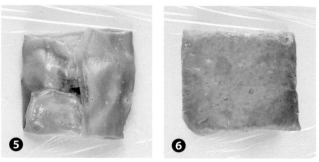

How to pack the bento

Unwrap the Omurice and place it seam-side down in the center of the box on a bed of greens. Tuck fruit into one side of the Omurice, partitioning with leaves. Place some Carrot and Tuna Salad and Tomato-marinated Eggplant on the other side of the Omurice. (They have compatible flavors, so no need to separate.) Cut an "X" into the top of the Omurice and fold back the flaps of egg to reveal the rice inside.

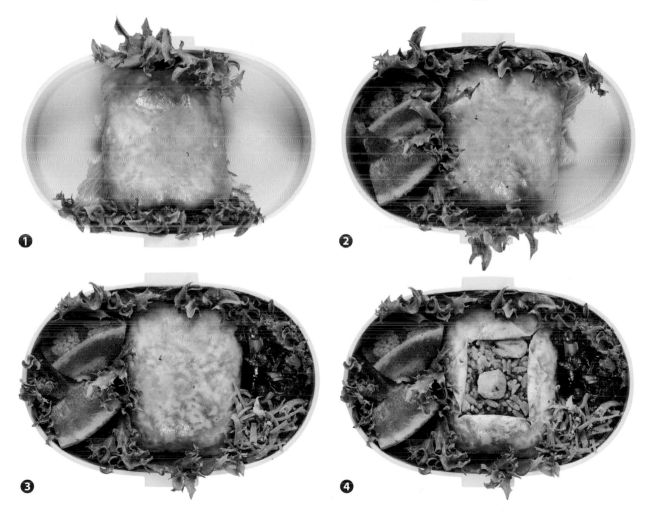

Index

Resources

ONLINE

Amazon.com is a great resource in any country to pick up everything from kitchen utensils to bento boxes, to Japanese ingredients. I have a curated list of some of my recommendations here: www.amazon.com/shop/norecipes

US

www.tokyocentral.com
www.nijiyashop.com/index.html

UK

www.japancentre.com/en

Global
anything-from-japan.com

OFFLINE
US

www.nijiya.com
mitsuwa.com
www.marukai.com

Acknowledgments

Maki: I would like to send my heartfelt thanks to my parents for sharing their wonderful recipes with me and for introducing me to the joyful art of cooking. Much love to my husband, Yoh, and sons, Kai and Hal, for warmly and patiently watching as I honed my bento making skills, and for ALWAYS being my No.1 fans. To my friends, thanks for being on the lookout for my new bentos, and for always being supportive of my dreams. To the staff at Bento Expo, thank you for inviting me on such a great television show. To Marc, thank you from the bottom of my heart for your helpful suggestions and advice. To Cathy and the staff at Tuttle Publishing, thank you so much for giving me such a wonderful chance and for being ever so patient with my English!

Marc: This book has been decades in the making, and there are too many people to thank individually. Still, for every muse, mentor, and fan out there who has inspired, guided, and supported me, please know that you have my gratitude and appreciation.

Mom, I want to thank you for never failing to have a hot comforting meal on the table at 6pm, regardless of how busy you were. Jerry, you're the only recipe follower in the family, but your food is consistently good, so thank you for teaching me the power of rigorous documentation. Dad, thanks for introducing me to cuisines from around the world, it not only inspired me to cook, but it also drove a desire to visit those far-flung places in person. Jim, you more than anyone inspired me to cook without recipes with your treasure-trove of sauces, spices, jams and chutneys.

Eric and Christina, thank you for giving me the opportunity to write this book. Cathy, Ann, and the rest of the team at Tuttle, thanks for your patience with this first time author. To Koide-san, Kumata-san, Shinohara-san, and Hanako-san, thank you for giving me a platform to share Japanese bento culture with the world. To Inaba-san, Otomo-san, Dora, and the rest of the Bento Expo crew, thank you for making every shoot run smoothly.

Aiko, thank you for being my partner in the kitchen, in business, and in life! Last but not least: Ayu, I want to send you a special thank you for making every day a new and exciting adventure!

Books to Span the East and West

Our core mission at Tuttle Publishing is to create books which bring people together one page at a time. Tuttle was founded in 1832 in the small New England town of Rutland, Vermont (USA). Our fundamental values remain as strong today as they were then—to publish best-in-class books informing the English-speaking world about the countries and peoples of Asia. The world is a smaller place today and Asia's economic, cultural and political influence has expanded, yet the need for meaningful dialogue and information about this diverse region has never been greater. Since 1948, Tuttle has been a leader in publishing books on the cultures, arts, cuisines, languages and literatures of Asia. Our authors and photographers have won many awards and Tuttle has published thousands of titles on subjects ranging from martial arts to paper crafts. We welcome you to explore the wealth of information available on Asia at **www.tuttlepublishing.com.**

Published by Tuttle Publishing, an imprint of Periplus Editions (HK) Ltd.

www.tuttlepublishing.com

Copyright ©2020 Periplus Editions (HK) Ltd

ISBN: 978-4-8053-1567-5

22 21 21   5 4 3

Printed in Malaysia   2102TO

TUTTLE PUBLISHING® is a registered trademark of Tuttle Publishing, a division of Periplus Editions (HK) Ltd.

Distributed by

North America, Latin America & Europe
Tuttle Publishing
364 Innovation Drive, North Clarendon, VT 05759-9436 U.S.A.
Tel: 1 (802) 773-8930; Fax: 1 (802) 773-6993
info@tuttlepublishing.com; www.tuttlepublishing.com

Japan
Tuttle Publishing
Yaekari Building 3rd Floor, 5-4-12 Osaki, Shinagawa-ku
Tokyo 141-0032
Tel: (81) 3 5437-0171; Fax: (81) 3 5437-0755
sales@tuttle.co.jp; www.tuttle.co.jp

Asia Pacific
Berkeley Books Pte. Ltd.
3 Kallang Sector #04-01, Singapore 349278
Tel: (65) 67412178; Fax: (65) 67412179
inquiries@periplus.com.sg; www.tuttlepublishing.com